Iswaydaarsi

5

Maxamed Xaashi Dhamac "Gaarriye" in World Poets' Tour with
Poetry Translation Center. Photo © by Crispin Hughes.

Maxamed Xaashi Dhamac
"GAARRIYE"

Biography and Poems

Edited by
Jama Musse Jama

2012

PONTE INVISIBILE
REDSEA-ONLINE.COM

REDSEA-ONLINE.COM Culture Foundation
Fidiyaha Aqoonta iyo Ereyga Dhigan - Xarunta dhexe
Daarta Oriental Hotel - Hargeysa, Somaliland
telephone: 00 252 2 525109 | 00 252 2 4099088
email: bookshop@redsea-online.com

Ponte Invisibile
Inquiries to the editor
Jama Musse Jama
Via Pietro Giordani 4, 56123 Pisa, Italy
www.ponteinvisibile.com
email: editor@redsea-online.com | editor@ponteinvisibile.com

Published by Ponte Invisibile (redsea-online), 2012, Pisa
I

Poems © Maxamed Xaashi Dhamac 'Gaarriye' 2012
Translations from the Somali © W. N. Herbert and Martin Orwin granted here by PtC
Translations from the Somali © David Harsent and Martin Orwin granted here by PtC
Translations from the Somali © Rhoda A Rageh
Photos © Crispin Hughes

First Edition 2012
Copyright © 2012 Ponte Invisibile Edizioni
A REDSEA-ONLINE Publishing Group Company.
ISBN 88-88934-33-2 | EAN 9788888934334

www.redsea-online.com/books

Suggested classification for the librarians
Maxamed Xaashi Dhamac "Gaarriye": Biography and Poems / Jama Musse Jama (edited by)
pp. 128 cm. 140x210
Includes Index and bilingual English-Somali poems.
ISBN 88-88934-33-2 EAN 9788888934334
I. Maxamed Xaashi Dhamac "Gaarriye" II. Biography and Poems III. Jama Musse Jama (edited by). Contributions by Martin Orwin, Abdirahman A. Farah, W. N. Herbert, Sarah Maguire, Mohamed Hassan "Alto", Rhoda A Raghe and David Harsent / IV. Biography / Literature / Poetry / Translations.

CONTENTS

INTRODUCTION: WHY THIS BOOK?

Jama Musse Jama

Maxamed Xaashi Dhamac "Gaarriye", one of the most famous living Somali speaking poets, was born, bred and brought up in Hargeysa, Somaliland. In the early 1970s, he was among many of his contemporaries living in Mogadishu whose works were regarded to have impact upon the prevalent socio-political situation in the country. They were mainly motivated and moved by their patriotic sentiments and leftist political bearing which was internationally popular in that era. Gaarriye was the initiator of the famous poetic combat chain better known as "Deelley" and the author of "Hagarlaawe", his collected poems, enough to establish his eminence as great poet among Somali speakers. His contributions to Somali literature and culture as a poet, scholar, liberal thinker and social personality over the past three gruesome decades are well recognised. Equally appreciated in no smaller measure are his indefatigable advocacy of human rights, freedom of thought and expression, and his vehement hatred of all forms of human degradation so brilliantly articulated in his poetry. In this regard, his master pieces on 'Nuclear Weapons', 'Nelson Mandela', 'Watergate' and 'Zimbabwe' readily spring to the mind. Well described by other scholars, Gaarriye "has been universally regarded as one of the most important Somali poets composing on a great variety of topics from nuclear weapons to Nelson Mandela. A poet who has never been afraid to engage in the politics through his poetry[..]" (PTC 2012).

Official censorship and its blatant harmful effect upon social justice were some of the main themes Gaarriye singled out for his unflinching poetic attack. So also his defence of peace was unreservedly forceful. In this regard, a historical instance worth citing was 30th April 1992, at a time when Somaliland was diabolically ravaged by civil strife. Gallantly taking his stand at the "Khayriya", the main public square of Hargeysa, he addressed the gathered masses lashing on the insanity of war and its horrific consequences. He reminded the gathered public of the immeasurable cost of losing their right senses demanding immediate cease fire and calling for peace. That was the hallmark of his famous poem "Ergo" (arbitrator). Here he never forgot, from the outset using his capturing style in reciting his poem, to mention the dictatorial era when before 10 years his poems had to run clandestinely fearing Siyaad Barre censorship, comparing it to that precious moment when he so proudly stood before them free from all strains to address them on such cardinal issues as the abnegation of war and the restoration of peace with its blessings.

Even before he fled to Ethiopia, joining the liberation movement, the dictatorial government had never been spared his bitter criticism. He starkly exposed its misdeeds and wrongdoings in the social affairs of the people. In fact some of his satirical works such as "Hashii Cosob", "Kabo Caseeye", "Madax Goodir", "Qiyaame", "Run", especially when recited in public, demonstrated further his ability as an extraordinary actor. With his familiar witticism in these poems and others equally incisive, he exposed the government's pathetic incompetence and the hollowness of its much vaunted system. The Somali masses never failed to grasp the essence of his message; and that was why he has always remained in the black books of the official establishment. When many of the then Somali lyrics composers became aligned with the government willing to please the dictatorship, he still used his sophisticated arm to defend the ethics and dignity of poetry, and he composed his piece "Qasab kuma balwayn karo" (*I can't be compelled to sing*).

By publishing this volume, our modest purpose is to celebrate this great poet's invaluable contribution to Somali culture and his instrumental role in setting a bridge to international literature. This volume is the fifth in the "Iswaydaarsi" (*Exchange*) series which aspires to translate Somali literature and wisdom into other languages, and at the same time provide specific knowledge of international classical literature to the Somali speaking readership. Gaarriye's translated poems into English fit well into the first category of books. His poems included in this volume are translated by Sarah Maguire, Mohamed Hassan "Alto", W. N. Herbert, Rhoda A Raghe, Martin Orwin, and David Harsent.

I am deeply thankful to Poetry Translation Center for their permission to reproduce in this publication all Gaarriye's poems they have translated as well as Herbert's article that appeared on their website. Some of the poems included here have already appeared in PtC's bilingual chapbook of Gaarriye's poems in Somali and English [PTC, 2012]. I am also thankful to the contributors of this volume, who with the limited time they had, yet so considerately managed to write about Gaarriye. Finally this publication would not have be possible without the support of the organizations Poetry Translation Center, Kayd Somali Culture and Arts and Redsea *Online* Culture Foundation.

Gaarriye with Sarah Maguire during the World Poets' Tour Photo C. Hughes

MAXAMED XAASHI DHAMAC "GAARRIYE": A SHORT NOTE OF BIOGRAPHY

Martin Orwin

Maxamed Xaashi Dhamac 'Gaarriye' was born in Hargeysa in 1949. He was brought up, following the break up of his parents' marriage, by an aunt Ruun Dhamac, and following her death, by a friend of hers, Biliso, who was a great influence on the young boy. Although from a poor background, various people helped him through his schooling which began at Biyo Dhacay Elementary School in Hargeysa and continued at Sheekh Secondary School where he excelled. In 1970 he went to Lafoole College near Mogadishu to read biology and following graduation worked as a teacher in various secondary schools until 1976 before returning to Lafoole as a lecturer in Somali literature. Shortly after this he was made the director of the Department of Somali Literature there and subsequently worked for the Academy of Science, Arts and Literature. Despite his formal training in biology, his role as an educationalist in literature stems from his early development as a poet and his deep interest and knowledge of Somali poetry. He also studied Arabic poetry at school and his work is influenced to some extent by such poets as Abu al-Qasim al-Shabby, Nizar Qabbani and the Abbasid poets. After 1982 he was involved in the opposition to the regime of Mohamed Siyaad Barre and lived for two years during this time in Abidjan, Ivory Coast. He currently works as professor of Somali literature in the Universities of Hargeysa and Amoud where his lectures on Somali poetry are very popular.

As a poet, he first came to prominence in the early 1970s contributing to the famous, long chain poem *Siinley* and writing poems on philosophical topics one such being *Garaad-daran* 'Self-misunderstood'. In 1971 he had been part of a group of poets who wrote the famous play *Aqoon iyo Afgarad* 'Knowledge and Understanding Language' which dealt with the theme of education. A sense of social engagement pervades Gaarriye's poetry; *Kabo-caseeye* 'Shoeshine Boy' (1979) is an example in which he ironically presents a malnourished, sore-ridden street boy who is whisked off the streets by the military so as not to 'offend' foreign dignitaries who have arrived in Mogadishu for events organized for the UNESCO International Year of the Child. Other poems demonstrated his international outlook such as the powerful *Wooter-gayt* 'Watergate' (1977), which deals with American foreign policy in light of the US veto against the newly independent Angola joining the United Nations; and a poem entitled *Maandheela* 'Mandela' (1980) which is a powerful support of Mandela and what he stood for at that time. Perhaps his most famous political poem is *Dugsi Ma Leh Qabyaaladi* 'Clanism Is No Shelter', which began a long and important chain of poems to which all the major poets of the time contributed and which became known as *Deelley* after the alliterative sound each poem followed.

Aside from his poetry, Gaarriye is known as the first to present the analysis of the metrical system of Somali poetry. In 1976 he published a seminal article in the national newspaper *Xiddigta Oktoobar* (October Star) which sets out three conditions for the metrical pattern known as *jiifto* which can then be applied analogously to other metrical patterns. These conditions relate to the patterning of long and short vowel syllables, the patterning of consonant clusters and doubled consonants, and word breaks. He has continued to think about these matters and has made further contributions, particularly on the matter of the role of certain consonants (virtual geminates) which behave like doubled consonants in the metre.

MAXAMED XAASHI DHAMAC "GAARRIYE": A HIGHLY TALENTED POET IN A NATION OF BARDS

Abdirahman A. Farah

I take real pleasure in being one of the very few lucky ones to have had such close acquaintance with the great poet Maxamed Xaashi Dhamac "Gaarriye" since we were toddlers attending the Quranic school together in Hargeysa in the mid fifties. Even in those early days, one never missed to notice laudable merits of his character. His intelligence, vivacious spirit, and gift of the gap were conspicuous to all around him, particularly his peers who expressed their appreciation by often swarming around him.

Moving to the intermediate and high school at Biyo Dhacay, he further revealed yet another commendable trait of his developing natural artistic qualities. His keen observation of details, avid reading and power of assimilation had been striking. Even his Arabic teachers were astonished with the ease and excellence he wrote his Arabic composition and how he won in every competition. This was reinforced by his fabulous memorisation of loads of verses of classical poetry both in Somali and Arabic which honestly revealed his singularity.

Strangely enough, it was at this same time in our high school he showed that his propensity for hard science and mathematics were not to be belittled or underrated when compared to his endowment in the faculty of art ; and in order to substantiate the seriousness of what he meant, he readily opted for biology as his major subject. But it was during his studies in Lafole Teachers' Training College in the 70s and later in the liberation struggle in the 80s that his literary production increased in leaps and bounds and brightly shown in the public arena. His major participation in the ground-breaking drama "Aqoon Iyo Afgarad" both in the production as well as the acting along with other literary stalwarts such as Maxamed Ibraahim Warsame "Hadraawi", Siciid Saalax Axmed and Muuse Cabdi Cilmi remains until this very day a house hold talk.

Not only content with dealing with domestic national problems, he had his fair share of addressing international burning issues of the day. His master piece on the horrors of war "Nabdaado", the nuclear menace to humanity as well as the ones on apartheid in South Africa titled "Nelson Mandela" followed by "Zimbabwe", "Watergate", all translated into English are highly acclaimed far and wide beyond the Somali frontiers. But undoubtedly, his most astonishing achievement is marked by his discovery of the principles upon which the whole range of the Somali poem is metrically based, "Miisaanka Maansada". Over the past century no literary feat of any hue had such a drastic positive effect upon Somali poetry as this outstanding revelation by this genius poet. To my great delight this unprecedented literary feat happened in 1976 immediately when I came back to Mogadishu after having completed my studies in Russia. The article on this subject appeared in the "Xiddigta Oktoobar" the Somali national daily newspaper and was rapturously received by the Somali literary circles.

His initiation of the famous poetic chain known as "Silsiladdii Deelley" in which he is joined by over 40 renowned poets of different shades and political stance is another glaring example of his pioneering role among the living Somali contemporary poets. Suffice it to say that Gaarriye's works are highly praised by distinguished scholars like G. W. Andrzejeweski, Muuse I. Galaal and Dr. Martin Orwin, teaching professor of Somali and Amharic in the School of Oriental and African Studies, of London University. The latter was so impressed by Gaarriye's immense contribution and literary stature that he voluntarily took upon himself the task of translating many of his poems. This magnificent gesture has further galvanised the friendly relations between these two worthy men of letters.

By way of conclusion, I would like to state that his prolific poetic production, and the various themes he deals with in his unique captivating style, coupled by his erudition are absolutely the main reason for the ever increasing number of young men and women, admirers who look up to him as their sole mentor and role model to emulate. Personally, I am very proud of our long standing intimate friendship I so cordially cherish.

Gaarriye with Martin Orwin during the World Poets' Tour.
Photo by C. Hughes

SOME THOUGHTS ON CO-TRANSLATING GAARRIYE

W N Herbert

The impact of Maxamed Xaashi Dhamac "Gaarriye" both as poet and person on my life and my work is more pervasive and more subtle than I can easily articulate, and I was saddened to hear of his current ill-health. I touch on his extraordinary generosity and hospitality in the following essay, but would like to add that it sparked a continuing fascination with his work and with Somali poetry and culture in general. For this I am deeply grateful, and I wish him as thorough a recovery as his condition allows. The poem 'Arrogance' was translated with Martin Orwin as part of the Poetry Translation Centre's 2008 project, but there wasn't room for it in the Enitharmon pamphlet – I am delighted that it's appearing here, where, for me, it stands as a harbinger for further translations I hope to embark on from the work of this great and internationally significant poet.

1. Arar *(Introduction)*

What a poet looks for in the act of translating from a language he or she doesn't understand differs slightly from what is sought by the creative translator of verse, working with a culture they know intimately, whether on a linguistic, literary or socio-political level. The difference, essentially, is that the didactic intention of the translator -their passion that others should know this poet, this form, this culture -is, for the poet, a self-directed and self-metamorphosing part of the process. That is, they wish to be changed by what they learn as technicians, as workers in the medium of verse. They want the new perspectives, the different handlings of tone and imagery, the shifts of emphasis in the metrical system, to affect and develop them as writers, not just as readers.

This learning-through-practice is, naturally, part of the translator's experience too, but poets are perhaps greedier, more selfish - a bit vampiric - and confined to fewer encounters, more prescribed contact. They can only discover what they need through interaction with an element the translator is well-versed in, which the reader encounters only by inference, and they themselves are generally ignorant of: the language. Through what they can be told about the host language, they begin to seek possibilities to address those issues - audience, symbol, metre - embedded within it.

So they are at once less than translators and more than readers. They are utterly dependent on the explications and guidance of their translator, who must function as both guide and ambassador ('dragoman' would be the Ottoman Greek term), and, where possible, the originating poet. But they are not quite as absolutely at the service of the reader as, ideally, the translator (and, presumably, that original poet) wishes to be. They, crucially, must be fed, nourished creatively by the process. This is fraught, tentative sort of work at the best of times: few who aim at mastery can leave their supposed status or their usual methods entirely at the door when entering the building, the city or the country of another's poem.

The best solution, I found, when working with Martin Orwin on the poetry of the great Somali writer, Maxamed Xaashi Dhamac 'Gaarriye', was to revert to the role of apprentice (not so far in my case). I joined the extensive band of what I learnt was Gaarriye's xer (his term plays, with self-deprecating mockery, on the idea of a band of disciples) - those students and former students I found, when visiting Somaliland, to be almost coterminous with the younger generation of writers and academics who are driving the two institutions of Hargeisa and Amoud universities, as well as gathering to exchange and perform their poetry at the huge, impromptu-seeming events that punctuated my stay.

Confronted with Somali -the language that 'makes Arabic look like Esperanto', as Sarah Maguire introduced it to me -I felt less the apprentice and more the schoolboy. And it was as a novice that I engaged with the practically-unique structural device at the heart of Somali poetry: the deployment of a single alliterative sound per (often lengthy) poem. This was, I discovered, a device which induces either virtuosity or failure. It was practically as a literary tourist that I experienced Somali culture's obsession with poetry, its groundedness in orality, so that most verse is still composed in the head rather on paper, and lives or dies in performance rather than in print; a culture where memory, first supplemented by the cassette, has now been augmented by the mp3, practically bypassing the book altogether. And it was certainly as a student (perhaps in my first year of PPE) that I found out about a complex political background: world opinion on the Somali situation, much distracted by lurid headlines, is informed by very few of the facts.

If I graduated at all from this compressed process - which took me from complete beginner to co-translator of four substantial poems (key to understanding Gaarriye's ground-breaking early career) within two months; and in nine months from someone who only knew of Somaliland from an old stamp collection to a dazzled, smitten visitor - it was with a Gentleman's Third. If I managed that much, it was because of the more-than-generous, exemplary instruction and truly scholarly collaboration offered by Martin; and by the teasing, revelatory openness and extraordinary hospitality of Gaarriye, who welcomed me to his poetry and his home with equal zest. It was all, as he often insisted with an emphatic wave of his hand, 'the Somali way'.

2. Dhexdhexaad *(Middle Section)*

How Martin and I worked on these pieces was, essentially, that I would stumble through each poem line by line, while he gave me a summation of its meaning, rhythm and role in relation to the whole poem, and the poem's place in Gaarriye's work as a whole. We would meet up each weekend and work our way intensively through the poems like this, setting his painstaking literals against Gaarriye's Somali and retranslating the latter phrase by phrase, with me taking away his and my notes, and trying to work up a fluent draft before our next meeting.

From that process (still ongoing, albeit in a less intense form, and still as challenging, as rewarding), I learnt three things which, as required, informed my own practice and may well change it. These should all have been self-evident from the outset, but, sometimes it's only by bumping your head repeatedly off a wall that you get a feel for its texture as well as its location.

In relation to the form of Somali poetry, I found that attempting a close match of single sound alliteration was crippling for the simple reason that this mode is no longer culturally dominant in English poetry in the same way that it is in Somali. The place given to alliteration in Anglo-Saxon and Middle English verse we have subsequently given to rhyme. How an alliterative poetry like that of Wales or Irish or Scottish Gaelic would handle the same problem is an interesting area for speculation. But to alliterate on one sound to this degree in English is to hark back less to Beowulf's bard than to the wail of the broadsheet, where headlines bash their message home by the same method. What in Somali is a musical note has become the clanging of an unsubtle bell.

I therefore found myself emphasising key alliterative word at key moments, but falling back on secondary alliterative groupings at other points, to honour the device but allow some degree of modulation in its execution. Thus, in 'Aadmi

(Arrogance),' which alliterates on the vowels (which I've narrowed down to A), most of the initial tercets have at least one significant alliterative word - 'Adam', 'awe,' 'air,' 'abyssal,' acacia' - but those which don't, usually alliterate in some other way: 'The camel's old keen for her calf,/be hushed and hear it...'.

In relation to imagery, as the previous example suggest, there is in Somali poetry a continuing emphasis on the rural and nomadic which reflects how most of the population lives at one point or another in the seasons or in their lives. It's difficult, without copious footnotes, to indicate to a predominantly urban readership the complex symbology of livestock, familial interrelations and particularities of weather which informs this poetry. Such a reader is in danger of seeing an indistinguishable mass of camels and dryness, and losing the fine gradation of perceptions which sit behind an ordinary Somali word like *saxansaxo*: the scent and coolness carried on the wind from a place where it is raining to a place where it is not.

Because Gaarriye's work is suffused with such distinctions, and because Martin and I knew we were preparing texts as much for performance as for the page - pieces which might have to resolve something of themselves in an instant as well as yield more upon reflection - we sought out solutions which had the ring and rhythm of proverbial utterance, but without sacrificing detail. Thus in 'Uurkubbaale (Seer),' we emphasised a proverbial feel where possible, '"A cloud in the east means rest your feet,/the rain will trek to us..."' and, where a lot of information had to be given, we did our best to keep the tone colloquial: '[a poem] is the finest matting, woven for a bride,/ the one the song calls "Refuser of poor suitors".'

In relation to the genre these long, loping poems fall into, designed as they are to be heard by large audiences, I found myself describing them to friends as 'non-lyric.' By this I meant, not that they failed to be lyrical in either their thought or their musicality (actually, they succeeded, often compellingly so), but that they were manifestly not reliant, as much of our poetry is, on a device of romantic intimacy: one person deploying that musicality to 'sing' to another, with the reader either pretending to overhear, or to be the person addressed.

As I saw in Somaliland, looking out on audiences in their hundreds, raucous in their delight at Gaarriye's driven, witty performances, these are not poems which need to pretend to have listeners, and the particular way in which they are 'public' has interesting ramifications for both the translating poet, and the attentive Western audience. I'd like to expand on these, both in terms of their relevance to the translation process and the broader set of influences upon the translating poet, for the rest of this piece.

***

As Martin argues in his important essay 'On the Concept of "Definitive Text" in Somali Poetry', the Somalis' veneration of poetry manifests itself in a fastidiousness about the accuracy of the recital, or, more precisely, a fastidious intent to be accurate:

> 'The performance of *maanso* is not something to which the reciter brings an affective contribution...it is the words which are of primary importance as is the painting rather than the frame. In other words the nature of the act of performing *maanso* is something which foregrounds the words themselves...the fact that variations may be found [in performance] does not detract from the central concept of the goal of verbatim memorization which implies the presence of the conception of a definitive text in the mind of the Somalis. The fact that the composer of the poem must always be acknowledged supports this.'

This respect for an integrity the poem is understood to possess in an a-textual state, that is, without the need for it ever to appear in print, is manifested specifically as an awareness of its content (as well as its formal integrity and the ownership of its author). Such respect, in itself, points to an interesting definition of 'public poetry'. Somali poetry is not public simply because it is addressed to a plural audience in a public setting. It is public because all its premisses of persona, form, tone and subject are to a marked extent shared by both poet and audience.

What the Somali poet is performing, in terms of subject, can seem more varied than our lyric mode; the politics of protest, for instance, play an honoured role, and the poem 'Geeridii Ina Boqor (Death of a Princess),' for instance, offers a trenchant critique of Saudi society. But, crucially, how it is performed must conform structurally to that shared pool of knowledge: a Somali audience traditionally heckles two types of failure: that of the alliteration and that of the metre.

All this impacts in two main ways on Western poets and their audiences. The first is that these structural certainties support length - arguments and images can be developed, instances can be enumerated: in short, rhetoric can be deployed as a performative as well as an argumentative principle.

When I was working on these pieces, I asked Martin whether the frequent divisions within a text corresponded to stanzas. He said they did not, and I began to think of them instead as simple verse paragraphs. Then, when I heard Gaarriye and other Somali poets read, I discovered that these short gaps were actually spaces for audience appreciation. As some rhetorical or imagistic or alliterative flourish was presented, which the poet knew would appeal to his audience, he paused for applause. This 'interruption' of the poem occurs very infrequently during a reading in the UK, though any poem which, without such pauses, is felt to go on too long, is often criticised as too 'rhetorical'. Gaarriye's example calls us to reconsider such terms.

In translating him, we had to begin with a premiss that each poem required as much rhetorical integrity and argumentative force as possible to sustain the attention of a Western audience. Each of those pauses, for instance, had to become as syntactically neat as possible. In 'Garaad-daran (Self-misunderstood),' I therefore embellished each of the iterations of the refrain 'Garaad-daran naftaydaay!' with a new term:

I can't understand you, curious self...
I can't get to grips with you, gregarious self...
I can't seem to fix you, quarrelsome self...
I can't get to grips with this garrulous self...

This allowed me to emphasise either the alliterative sound (G), or bring out the play of puns and near-puns on his own name Gaarriye comes up with in this poem on the growth of a poet's mind. Then, with Martin's cautious approval, I added a summative element just before the conclusion, to give that Western listener a firmer handle on this poem of length: 'Curious, gregarious, garrulous self,/did you fail to grasp the stifling norms?/To quarrel...'.

Ironically, given this, our only major deviation, the second main impact of the Somali sense of 'definitive text' on our translation was in terms of integrity. Just as another Somali, reciting someone's poem, must provide the author's name and aim for 'verbatim memorization,' to use B.W. Andrzejewski's term, so, for a translator from Somali, textual accuracy is a higher than usual priority. This is one case in which the version, for a frequently bilingual Somali audience, decidedly will not do. Martin and I therefore agreed that (with certain clearly-argued exceptions!) following the meaning took priority over such gestures as attempting, for instance, to find a consistent rhythmic equivalent.

3. Gebaggebo *(End)*

When a horse walks into a bar, joke logic compels the barman to ask, 'Why the long face?' Perhaps the same is true of camels, but when a poet walks into the same establishment, the barman feels at liberty to protest, 'Why the long poem?' Therefore for me, as a committer of poems which occasionally go 'over the page,' this issue of the rhetorical integrity of a substantial 'public' poetry, was of great personal value. It was the element which fed me creatively.

I had noticed, when Gaarriye and I first read together, in Liverpool's Bluecoat Centre, that the large Somali audience were not content to sit still, to be rapt as the master rapped. On the contrary, they clapped, exhorted, got up, took photos with their mobiles, posed in those photos with Gaarriye, called people up, asked Gaarriye to speak to those people, or attempted to capture him reciting down the line. Through all this he indefatigably, indeed insouciantly, continued to perform - and therefore so did I.

In other words I learnt that the well-made poem is sufficiently robust. If it is very well-made, it induces applause and, here and there, that rapt look occurs for real, not through politeness. It doesn't require our reverence or more polite forms of appreciation, only the space in which to, as Martin says, 'foreground the words'. Everything else is background noise. Supplementing this insight, the Somali sense of the 'integrity' of the poem was of equal importance to me as a teacher of my own, not very xer-like, body of students. I've been looking for a long time for a way of describing the strange manner in which a poem exists at each stage up to the point of publication. That ghost shape which haunts the head, perhaps accompanied by a title or the hollow frame of a stanza, perhaps not; those few scraps and fragments that hang around, sometimes for years, waiting for major drafting to be done; the working draft that undergoes major or minor changes as a result of (or in defiance of) feedback from a peer or mentor - in each case there is a sense of a gravitational centre, something which it is necessary for the composing poet if no-one else to believe in as the 'poem'. It has always seemed too premature a moment to apply the term 'text' to this fluid entity, with all the theoretical issues which haunt that term. But the Somali sense of a goal to which the recited poem is constantly aspiring strikes me as a more evolved idea of a similar type. 'Text' in this context becomes a post hoc rationalisation, a concept to which we might prefer this aspiration of a particular confluence of language and metric patterning to achieve structural coherence.

Between these two nutritious revelations, I feel I've experienced a feast of words and experiences which will enrich my practice for some time to come. As it says at the (temporary) close of 'Uurkubbaale' (the poem is in two halves of which, so far, we have only translated the first):

> Dear God, don't seal this man's lips —
> may the truth he speaks continue
> as though it burst fro my own mouth.

(*) Traditionally, *maanso* is the most consciously literary mode of Somali poetry; Martin notes in 'On the Concept of "Definitive Text" in Somali Poetry': 'a maanso poem is considered to be constructed in three parts: *arar*, *dhexdhexaad* and *gebaggebo*, which we might translate as "introduction", "middle section" and "end" respectively.'

Gaarriye with W. N. Herbert during the World Poets' Tour. Photo C. Hughes

Gaarriye in tour with Poetry Translation Center in World Poets' Tour.
Photo C. Hughes

Gaarriye with Hussein Bissad, the second tallest man in the world, a fellow
Somalilander. Photo C. Hughes.

Gaarriye in tour with Poetry Translation Center invites to the stage the second tallest man in the world, a fellow Somalilander. Photo C. Hughes.

SELECTED POEMS

MANDELA

Maxamed Xaashi Dhamac 'Gaarriye'

The literal translation of this poem was made by Martin Orwin and
Maxamed Xasan 'Alto'. The final translated version of the poem is by
David Harsent.

The poem is under my hand.
The images crowd my head.
Poetry is the way
To get this story told.
Poetry has the strength
To tell the story well,
As long as the images hold,
As long as the poem writes.
The Oppressor comes into court.
He is the Prosecutor,
He is the Judge and Jury;
There is no 'win or lose' -
The case is cut and dried.
The Defendant stands alone.
The Prosecutor calls
Himself as Witness - yes,
The Judge upholds the law
That he himself created:
It changes as he chooses.
The Jury only knows
One word - the word is 'Guilty'.
This poem is a gun.
This poem's an assassin.
Images mob my mind...
This pen's a spear, a knife,

MANDHEELA

Maxamed Xaashi Dhamac 'Gaarriye'

Gabay-yahaw i maqal;
Madax-yahaw rimmani
Jiiftada madiix;
Masafooy gadood;
Maax-yahay ha gudhin.

Inta uu mudduci
Madal-weyne yimi,
Wax kastuu marsado
Marlay kiiska qabo;
Oo maddaacalii
Maanshaa Allee,
Garta madax ka yahay
Ka markhaati yahay
Sharcigana matalo,
Madfac-yahaw ha damin;
Mujrim-yahaw ha ladin;
Maskax-yahay godlani
Maansada ha dayn.

Qalin-yahaw mindiyo
Ii noqo maddane;
Ku marriimo dhiig;
Kuna maydho ciin.
Khadkan hoo murka ah;
Kii macallinka ah

A branding-iron, an arrow
Tipped with righteous anger.
It writes with blood and bile.

I take this bitter ink,
Blood-red, to make my mark;
Corruption from the wound,
Sap from the poison-tree,
Aloe and gall and myrrh.
This poem's a loaded gun,
This verse a Kalashnikov.
I aim it at the snake
That slithers to our children
And strikes! See where the tell-tale
Blood-beads pearl on the skin.
The snake, the Prosecutor,
The Oppressor, the Judge, the Jury -
You must always aim for the head.
This poem is a gun
And words are ammunition.
This poem tells a story
That can't be cut or censored.
This poem's not up for sale,
It can't be bought as men
And cattle can be bought,
So don't make me an offer,
Put your money back
In your purse... But you can listen,
Everyone can listen,
Not just the great and good,
Not just Nelson Mandela.
Judge and Jury, listen!
Prosecutor, listen!
Policeman, come and listen!
Turnkey, come and listen!
You who perjure, listen!

Ee midab-caska ah.
Ku dhig heestan milil;
Maaleey qadhaadh
Dacar lagu margado.
Maarrahaan sitiyo
Kalaashkoofka mudan,
Midig aad tartide
"Madad" baan ku idhi.
Maska ubadka jaray
Dhiiggana ku mamay
Ila moora-duug.

Murti iyo higgaad
Maxlal aan ku dhalan,
Ninna macasha qaban
Waa meeqa odhan,
Ku macsuun tix aan
Maamuus ku ladhay,
Maandheela iyo
Muudaaga xumi
Dad wuxuu makalay;
Ama reer muskood
Kaga dhigay maxbuus.

Afartaa miscirir
Mus-duleed u daa.

Mid kaleeto waa
"Maqaleey war-laay
Ma laguu warramay?"

Waxaan ahay madluun
Godobtiisa maqan,
U maleegan oo
"Maya" yidhi dulliga
Waan miigganahay;

You who torture, listen!
I want you to hear this poem;
I want you to hear me speak
As if I were Mandela.
I speak for him - Mandela.
I speak for an angry man,
A man whose voice was stopped,
A man whose mouth was gagged
Because he once said, 'No!'
'No!' to the Prosecutor,
'No!' to the Judge and Jury,
'No!' to injustice, 'No!'
To indignity and oppression.
He says, 'Don't think I'm beaten;
Don't think of me as weak
Or wretched. I'm no slave.
I'm not destitute
Although they stole from me.
I'm not without a home
Although my land's been taken.
Don't pity me; don't tell me
I'll have my chance at glory.
Didn't Jesus ask us
To turn the other cheek
And give the Fool who slaps us
Another chance to show us
Just how much he hates us?
And if that Fool should kill me:
Tell me, who's the victor?
He thinks of me, that man,
As someone who has no one:
No friends, no family,
No allies, no supporters.
He cannot see the circle -
Right round the globe - of people,

Nin mannaagayoo
Macaluul darteed
Milgo-beelayoo,
Maalkiisa dhacan
Marti inu ku yahay
La marsiinayiyo,
Mana ihi miskiin,
Ninna muuno iyo
Naxariis ka mudan.

Nacas muruq is-biday
Markuu dhabanka bidix
Farba meel ku dhigo,
Sidii Nabi Masiix
Dhanka midig u dhiib,
Mawd baan ka xigay.
Ninka midho-yariyo
Madi garab lahayn
Ii malaynayiyo
Muska tiidsanee
Igu meersanee
Madaw iyo cadba leh,
Een mawqifkiyo
Mitidkaanu nahay,
Ku midaysan nahay,
Kala maan ahaa.

Uurkayga madhan
Muruqyada i fagan,
Murugada naftiyo
Dabarkaygu maran,
Mucsurkaan qabaa,
Waa miino iyo
Meleg aasanoo,
Mar inay qarxaan
Ku muddaysanoo,

All races, colours, creeds,
Calling out for justice.
If I say I'm hungry
I mean hungry for justice.
If I say I'm hog-tied
I mean hog-tied by lies.
If I say I'm blind,
I'm blind to compromise.
If I say an angel
Stands at my right shoulder
I mean 'Angel of Death',
I mean 'Death in Disguise'.
Everything I've suffered,
Everything I've dreamed of,
Are mine and mine alone.
The Judge and Jury know me.
They know what I have suffered.
They think that what I'm thinking
Is what they think I'm thinking.
It's not. If I say 'Angel'
I mean Angel of Death.
I mean the Angel's shadow
That darkens all my thinking.
The brush they use to sweep
My thoughts out of the door
Is worn down to the shaft.
Only the thoughts are left.
The snake-bite and the blood-beads,
The blood-beads and the poison,
Are my immunity.
Once my sleep was dreamless,
Once my mind was blank;
Now my dreams are rich,
My every thought is clear.
Now I see a way -

Wixii lay marshiyo
Waxan maaganahay
Kala maan ahaa.

Maanshee la yidhi
Xaaqinkaa murxee
Dhul madhaa ma jiro.

Miciyihi darraa
Ee igu mudnaa,
Mariidkiyo suntii
Maaradoodi helay;
Haddaan maahsanaa
Miyir-doorsanaa,
Miiraabay oo
Mugga waan il-baxay;
Majaraan hayaa,
Duul hore u maray,
Ay mahadiyeen.

Afartaa mullaax,
Uga maydhax-diir.

Mid kaleeto waa,
Hadal waa murtiye
Maqal Abu-hadroow.
Tixdu waa mag-dheba;
Nin kastoo mitida
Oo madiidin neceb,
Waa madhax u yaal;
Waa muuno iyo
Taallo aan u muday,
Maandheela iyo
Cidda uu matalo;
Magli baan ku qoray.

A way others have taken;
It's called the Road to Freedom.
I want you to hear him speak:
Hear Mandela's wisdom.
Listen, all who hear me,
All who think as I do.
Abu Hadra - hear me!
Poet and friend, now listen!
I know you'll understand.
This poem's a ransom-note,
Blood-money to the many
Who cry aloud for justice.
It's payback to Mandela
And everything he stands for
And everyone he speaks for.
This poem has a blade
Hidden at its heart.
That steel will last forever!
So listen, Abu Hadra!
If you will listen, others
Will listen too, will hear
The words as if Mandela
Was calling them to arms.
They'll grasp the blade that's hidden
Deep inside this poem;
They'll show the Jude and Jury
The cutting-edge of freedom;
They'll show the Prosecutor
The blade that lasts forever;
They'll never bow their heads
Or walk in chains and fetters.
This poem is a mirror
I've made for us, Hadraawi,
A mirror we can hold up
To show the ignoramus

Adna Maxamadoow
Maansadu nin geya,
Kama maarantee,
Mayalkeeda qabo;
Gumaystaha ku maag.
Madaxoo la rogo
Iyo midab-takoor,
Inaynaan mareeg
Marna qaadanayn,
Ninka mooggan iyo
Macal-cune dhacsii.
Miliqsade ka nixi.
Hal-muceedyadii
Mari aad tiqiin;
Oo mahadho iyo
Maahmaah ka reeb.
Kana marag ahaw
Rag hadday murmaan,
Mabda'eenu waa
Isagoon mugdiyo
Madmadoow ku jirin,
Maantiyo berriba
Malafsade ha dhaco;
Xalaal-maal ha jiro;
Dadku waa masee
Ha mudh-baxo cadligu

The depth of self-deception
That lies in his reflection;
To show the Judge and Jury
How the wide world sees them;
To show the man who takes
Pleasure in pain the guern
Of glee that warps his smile.
Hadraawi, read this poem
To anyone who'll listen.
Help them to find the voice
I've given to Mandela.
And tell them this: our purpose
Is peace; our password 'Freedom';
Our aim, equality;
Our way the way of light.

PASSING CLOUD

Maxamed Xaashi Dhamac 'Gaarriye'

The literal translation of this poem was made by Martin Orwin and
Maxamed Xasan 'Alto'. The final translated version of the poem is by
David Harsent.

Setting sun
You're on the run:
Late afternoon
And gone so soon!
What are you scared of? What's the rush?
Is it the spears of light that shine
Back at you from rock and bush?
Is it the dark creeping up on you
Or bad news from the depths of night
That makes you want to hide your light?
Or is it this girl, more beautiful
Than rain in the season of drought, whose grace
Is greater by far than the subtle pace
Of a passing cloud when it's nudged by the wind?
When you and she exchanged glances just now,
It was you who grew pale, it was you who shrank
From the gleam in her eye and the glow of her smile.
Setting sun
You're on the run:
Late afternoon
And gone so soon!
Have you gone
To warn the moon
That she must face
This greater grace?

FAD GALBEED

Maxamed Xaashi Dhamac 'Gaarriye'

Gabbal-dhaca cadceed-yahay
U sii faano-guratee
Casar gaaban liiqii
Godka weeraraysaa!
Go'e fuley miyaad tahay?
Waa maxay garmaamadu?

Ma googooska sagalkiyo
Gamasyada shucaacaa
Gaade kaa horreeyiyo
Gurigaad ku hoyan layd
War ku gubay ka soo direy?

Mise gabadhan dhoolkiyo
Gu'goo shaalka xaytiyo
Fad galbeed la moodaa
Kolkaad gelin is-dhugateen
Guluubkaagii shiikhoo
Dib-u guradku waa baqe?

Mise ganac-jabkaagiyo
Waxaad galabta mudataad
Intay goori goor tahay
Dayax soo lug-gu'i laa
Sii war-geli is-leedahay?

The roll of the clouds, the furl of the waves -
A sea of cloud stained purple and red,
The swing of her arms, the swing and the sway
Of her hips as she walks is just like the way
You sway and dip and the end of the day.
Now the clouds turn their backs on you.
They only have eyes for the eyes of the girl:
Eyes that launch love-darts, darts that sink
Into the flanks of the clouds and draw
Droplets of blood that stain the sky.
Setting sun
You're on the run:
Late afternoon
And gone so soon…
These are the lines
That seemed to fall
To hand when first
I saw the girl.
Now this is what
I most recall:
The way she reached up to gather fruit
Believing herself to be alone
Until she saw me there, wide-eyed,
As the wind read my mind and sent a gust
To part her dress and lay her breast
Bare for the space of an indrawn breath.
Ah, yes, I remember that…and the way
She caught at the cloth and fastened it,
Turning her face from mine, her eyes
Lowered, as if to say: No man
Has seen before what you saw today.

Gedgeddoonka hirarkee
Iyagoo garaaro leh
Gaatin-socodka laafyaha
Xarragada u gaarka ah
Goonyahaaga tiiciyo
Gaardiga daruuraha
Kugu gaaf-wareegee
Gumucaad ridaysiyo
Goolli-baadh fallaadhaha
Shafka kaga garaacdee
Isu rogay guduudkee

Dhiiggooda gobo'liyo
Giirgiirka caadka leh
Ku sibbaaqday guudkiyo
Gara-saar-dabtoodii
Maxaa maanta gaasirey?
Miyay kugu giriifeen?

Mise waxay ka giigeen
Gobaad haybaddeediyo
Gantaalaha jacaylkiyo
Kalgacaylka beereey
Indhaheedu ganayaan?

Afartaa siddiri-gam
Waxaan gocanayaa weli

Tiiyoo gareyskiyo
Marta debec u gunuddoo
Guranaysa hoobaan
Oo aan geyaankeed
Geesaha ka filanayn
Dabayshii gadoodee
Uurkayga garatee
Gaadmada ku qaaddee
Gosha iyo horaadkiyo

Gaaddada u faydiyo
Garba-duubka maraday
Durba "geb" isku siisiyo
Gabbashada xishoodka ah
Gorodday lulaysiyo
Ugubnimo-gandoodkii.

SEER

Maxamed Xaashi Dhamac 'Gaarriye'

The literal translation of this poem was made by Martin Orwin. The
final translated version of the poem is by W N Herbert.

In my cradle I heard the women sing
'In the name of God, "Yaasin"':
this is how we begin,
with the dance step and the dance.
I was playing 'biito biiti',
singing 'Bille-jire'–
this is how Gaarriye grew.

I suckled on hearsay, drank in lore:
'A cloud in the east means rest your feet,
the rain will trek to us.'
Dear friend, dear Burhaan, I was taught
there are two types of poem:
that which tells you how things are
and that with another agenda –
the people know which is which.

When she brought me up, Biliso said,
'If a poem is a farm
then how things truly are, that's water;
the best words for the best thoughts,
that's how it begins.
Justice is your only compost,
life itself is what you hoe:
just squeeze truth from what happens
and in its own time it will sprout.

UURKUBBAALE

Maxamed Xaashi Dhamac 'Gaarriye'

'Cawdu billoo balooy baydh.'
'Bismillaahi "Yaasiin"'.
Botorkiyo ciyaartoo
Sidaa lagu bilaaboo,
Anna biito-biitiyo
Bille-jire ku dheelaan
Beri hore garaadsaday.

Dadka waxan ka bawsaday:
'Dhool bari ka hirey baa
Dhaanka loo bariiyaa'.
Gabaygana Burhaanoow
Waxa aniga lay baray
Inu laba u kala baxo
Beeshana u kala yahay:

Waxay Biliso igu tidhi:
'Hadday maanso beer tahay
Run baa lagu biyeeyaa.
Bilicsiga dareenkaa
Lagu baalaleeyaa;
Xaq baa lagu bac-rimiyaa.
Baaqbaaqa noloshiyo
Biyo-dhiijinteediyo
Xilligay ku biqishaa.

'Whether a poem brings forth seeds
depends on how it's tended and by whom –
the spot in which it's planted;
depending on who needs it and for what
its husk is hulled or boiled.

'A poem is the measure for
that trek beneath the draining sun
each generation adds to;
when you have to stand and fight
it shows you where to point the gun.

'It guides you like a conch shell horn,
the call of the large camel bell;
it is the words' own bugle.
It is the finest matting, woven for a bride,
the one the song calls 'Refuser of poor suitors'.
It's not sold for coppers,
it's not for praising the powerful;
to put a price on it, any price,
cheapens it and is forbidden.

'It's riding bareback on an unbroken horse –
you don't hobble its heels.
Those who fear for their hides
and won't ride without a saddle,
those lacking in the craft, can't get near this:
lies have nothing to do with it.
Poetry is a woman you do not betray,
to abuse her beauty is a sin.'

* * *

'It's most lovely when most perfectly timed,
as though, met at morning,
you exchanged greetings
at just the right moment.

'Midho waxay u bixisaa
Habka loo barbaarshiyo
Barta lagu abqaalaa.
Sida loogu baahdaa
Loo buushe-bixiyaa;
Ama loo bislaystaa.

'Waxa lagu bardaanshaa
Baqoolkiyo geeddiga
Fac kastaa intuu bogo.
Bullashada dagaalkana
Bunduqay tilmaantaa.

'Waa buun wax lagu hago;
Boodaanta yeedhmada
Bigil ereygu leeyahay.
Caws baar leh weeyaan;
Lana baxay sabool-diid
Soddon laguma baayaco.
Boqor laguma caabudo.
Biidhi-qaatennimiyo
Baqas waa ka xaaraan.

'Waana biime liidda ah,
Boqnihiisa lama xidho.
Nin baqdaa ma halabsado;
Bayd-gaabku kuma galo;
Beentana wax kuma laha.
Waa Bilan ma-geyno ah;
Bog-dooxeedu waa sino.'

* * *

'Waxay bilic wax dheer tahay;
Iyadoon bariidada
Ballankeedi ka hor dhicin,
Kolkay bocorta maansado,

When your own wings feel so bedraggled
that you need another's touch,
then the full beauty of a poem
is like a butterfly meeting
a just-wakened flower
at the exact moment of dawn.

'When it seems to caress your flank,
to massage a salve into you;
when the pupil of its arrow pierces you
striking the mark exactly,
splitting your anguished cries in two.
Like a seer who peers inside you,
it homes in on your over-sensitivities,
your innermost wounds.

'When you suddenly hear of your betrothal
it sends the message deeper
into your most vulnerable point.
Poetry is the mine-seeker
opening your old, scarred-over hurt,
discovering your untouched earth,
that place closed off
from those closest to you.

'When Baahi-laawe, that dancing verse,
brushes the melancholy from you
as though it were a dust
that settled on your lust for life,
choked the desire in your chest;
it's like a grenade, a bomb,
its blast-range perfectly judged
so each stanza touches you
from problematic top to troubled toe,
exploding from your core.

Adoo baalku kaa qoyey
Xadantana u baahnaa,
Sidii baalalleey iyo
Balanbaallis qalimo leh,
Ooy ubax baraarugay
Isku waa-bariisteen.

'Bogga kuu salaaxdee
Burcad kuugu duugtee,
Bu'da leebka kugu mudan
Baydari-abbaartee,
Bulxankeedu laba-dhaca
Sida uur-ku-baalaha,
Boogahaaga hoosiyo
Bayrtaada qoomee.

'Kolba baaq xiloodin ah
Barta aad u nogoshahay
Intuu baac u sii dego,
Tixda miino-baadhkii
Fiix kugu biskootiyo
Dhul bacdii ku taal iyo,
Ku banayso meel aan
Beryahaaba gacal dayin.

'Ee baahi-laawuhu
Adigoo basiiro leh
Intuu boodhka kaa tumo,
Xiisaha basaasiyo
Beer-qaado laabtee,
Tuduc wali gun iyo baar
Meel baas ku taabtee,
Intuu baaxad le'eg yahay
Isagoo banbaane ah
Badhtankaaga ka sanqadho.

'When it permeates you
each time a line is recited
as though from a secret page
on which your own secrets are exposed
so that each time you scan it
you jolt with anxiety.'

This poem alliterates in 'b'
but all the best poems are branded
so that each page which is turned
makes you believe you've confessed
and each time your soul
involuntarily cries out, 'Bravo!
Dear God, don't seal this man's lips –
may the truth he speaks continue
as though it burst from my own mouth.'

'Ee kugu ballaadhee
Markii bayd la sheegaba,
Sidii baal qarsoodi ah
La bac dhabay xogtaadii,
Hadba baallo-daymada
Faraq-bood ka qaaddee.'
Maansada ba'leeyda ah
Ee baadi-soocda leh,
Bog kastoo la soo rogo
Sir aad bixisay mooddee,
Nafta oo baraad li'i:
Kolba 'baga!' tidhaahdiyo,
'Bishmaha Eebbe kuma jaro.
Ninka yidhi run badanaa!
Ma afkaygu kala baxay?'

SHE

Maxamed Xaashi Dhamac 'Gaarriye'

The literal translation of this poem was made by Martin Orwin and
Maxamed Xasan 'Alto'. The final translated version of the poem is by
David Harsent

Is she milk, is she more, is she buttermilk?
Is she bread, is she bread and milk, is she?
Would you say she's good luck? Would you say
She's a riddle, or maybe the answer?
Is she kindness or thought when it's solemn?
Is she thought, is she more - an idea?

Is she clouds that give rain, clouds that gather,
Clouds that bless, clouds that crowd, clouds that linger?
Would you say she's good luck, would you say
She's the pattern of stars struck at nightfall
When the day will bring cloudwrack and rainfall?

Would you say she's green growth in the rainfall?
Would you say she's the sun in the morning
That soaks up the dew, that disperses
The mist? Is she water that gathers
In pools after rain? Is she moonlight
Reflected in pools? Is she starlight
So bright when it floods with the moonlight
That you're blind to the land that you stand on?

Would you say she's green growth that the rainfall
Has washed and made sweet? Is she water
That lies on the land like a blessing?
Is she herself sweet, is she shapely?
Is her sweetness the perfume of water?

CARSHIGII JAMAALKA

Maxamed Xaashi Dhamac 'Gaarriye'

Ma cawaa ma caanaa?
Ma cug baa ma cigashaa?
Ma ciirsaa ma calaf baa?
Ma cisaa ma culuq baa?
Ma daruur gu' curatoo,
Cir caddaad an noqon baa?
Ma cigaalka feleggiyo,
Cirjiidkii Mariikh baa?

Ma magool cusayb baa?
Ma cadceed arooryoo,
Falaadhaha casuusta leh
Ku cabsiisay dheededoo
Ceeryaantii didisaa?
Ma xareed is celisaa?
Ma habeen cadda ah oo,
Balliyada cigaagani,
Casuumeen xiddigahoo,
Cirka dayaxi kaa jiray
Dhulka kaa cawaray baa
Cosob rayska xaadhiyo
Ma gargoorkii Ceeg oo
Calyayada barkaday baa?

Alla samay cuddoonaa!
Udugaa carfoonaa!

Is she beautiful, thoughtful and clever?
Does she live as she should? Does she honour
The qualities womanhood stands for?

You can see she's not weak and not foolish;
You can see she's not lazy and sluttish,
Not stubborn or sloppy or rowdy,
Neither a shrew nor a nag, she's
A woman who keeps a full larder,
A woman who'd greet you and feed you.

She's the lie of the stars that brings rainfall,
Not the set of the stars that brings drought to
The lie of the land that you stand on.

She's not fat, she's not thin, she is perfect.
She is modest - she dresses discreetly -
But it's clear that her body is perfect.

Oh, Cabdi, you see her as I do -
The way that she sways as she walks is
The reason I call her Catiya,
Catiya, whose walk is a rhythm
That chimes with my heart when I see her.

In the evening, she brushes her hair from
The crown to the tip and the breeze lifts
Each strand, so the eyes of the young men
Follow the stroke and the windblown
Hair as it catches the last of
The sun as it sets and makes firebrands,
Black but shot through with the sunset.

The colour of Catiya's skin is
The colour that all women envy.
Her eyes, soft and brown, are the eyes of
The desert gazelle, while her nose is

Samsam caynka loo dhigay
Citibaaro badanaa!
Callo ma aha liiti ah
Habac maaha ceebo leh
Qallaf maaha camal ba'an
Coon maaha loo hoyan
Baali maaha caaryaleh
Cirir maaha toomama
Cawro maaha socod badan
Cayil maaha laga dido
Caatana u may bixin.
Cid kastaba u geeyoo
Meel laga canaantiyo
Cillad loo ma heli karo.
Cabdiyow tallaabada
Cutiyaan idhaahdaa
Timahay caweyskii
Cirifyada u saartee
Ku cayaara leydhee
Cawryaan haldhaayadu
Indhaheeda cawsha ah
Mas cideedka midabka ah
Sanqaroorka caynaba
Timaheeda culayga ah
Ciridkeeda dhuxusha ah
Ilkahaa caddaanka ah
Camankeeda xaadda leh
Dhexda caara-dhuubta ah
Cududaha garaaraha
Kubabkay u culustahay
Cambarshaha surkeeday
Sirirsheen cabbaadhyadu
Waa Xuur al-Caynoo
Kolba anuu tin iyo cidhib
Cad aan quudho kuma arag.
Cagfudayd u may dhalan

Perfectly straight and her gums are
Black, black as charcoal. Oh, Cabdi,
The white of her teeth and the down on
Her cheek! Can you see how her waistline
Is curved like a spear; can you see how
Her arms make an elegant shape in
The air as she moves, how her calves flex,
How her neck, with its dapple of amber,
Lightly creases: the neck of a Houri.

There is nothing to fault in this woman,
Not a flaw to be found in her beauty.
She is never impatient or angry;
She never complains. Could you weary
Of a woman like that? She could never
Lie or be troublesome. No one
Ever spoke ill of this women:
Her soft speech, her quick mind, her modest
Way in the world - this young woman
Whose future, I know, will be brighter
By far than the star of the evening.

Oh, Cabdi, you see her as I do:
A child who is almost a woman,
In the very first flush of her beauty.
I praise her. I crown her with garlands.
Haadrawi, match my song with your song.

Cadho lagu ma sheegeyn
Waa canaadi lama odhan
Wax ka cawda maan arag!
Carrabkeedu beentiyo
Ma yaqaano caydaba
Wax ka cawda maan maqal
Ma cod dheera waa gabadh
Xishood baa u caado ah
Cimri waa u gaban weli
Caqli waa u waayeel
Cidhib baanay leedahay.

Aniguna ma caasiyo
Cadraddii ammaan lehe
Carshigii jamaalkaan
U caleemo saaraye
Adna cadar Hadraawow
Hambalyada u soo curi

DEATH OF A PRINCESS

Maxamed Xaashi Dhamac 'Gaarriye'

The literal translation of this poem was made by Martin Orwin and
Maxamed Xasan 'Alto'. The final translated version of the poem is by
W N Herbert

Xaye cala salaa
Come to prayer
Xaye cala falaax
Come to salvation
I can't remember
which prayer time it was
but I had to answer.
It may be the way of this world
beneath the witness of the stars
but last night I was told,
'They gorged on clotted blood.'

The earth there is dry and gleaming
scraped smooth
like camel fat.
All the goats and sheep
have grazed the land bare.

The place is ridden with ticks,
a desert where no-one can rest,
a scrubland sitting on oil;
floods of people with guns
and without restraints
surround it.

The place is duned,
with a humid wind;

GEERIDII INA BOQOR

Maxamed Xaashi Dhamac 'Gaarriye'

'Xaye cala salaa'
'Xaye calal falaax'
Xilli loo addimay
Ma xusuusan karo;
Xilna waa jiraa
Waana xaal-adduun;
Xiddigihi cirkana
Xalaa laygu yidhi:
"Xinjireey liqeen".

Dhulku wuu xarkagay
Sidii xuuko geel
Waanu xiiran yahay.
Xooluhu dhammaan
Waa xaaluf-daaq.

Xaggu waa qaniin
Xaggu lama-degaan;
Xidhku waa saliid,
Daad-xoor dab-liyo
Xadhig-lama-sitaan
Ku dul xeeran yiin.

Xaggu waa bacaad
Xanfar iyo dabayl;
Malaa waa xagaa.

it is, perhaps, the hottest time.

It is also cities
sprouting skyscrapers
which exhaust the eye,
furnished and fringed
with damask and silk;
they eavesdrop on air's gossip.
This is where those responsible
hoard their possessions.

Rivers flow within that land
waters of the Holy Places
and whisky foam
and froth up there.

The place is misery itself,
women burdened with children
hawking and gasping,
bearers and bricklayers
ground down and harassed.

My first quarter is done.
Look still more closely:
see our young woman, Xiis,
wholesome as a honeycomb,
born within the pale.
Like the choicest virgin mare,
she isn't bridled for
some camel raid, nor
a share of the loot.

She is Heaven's eye, a houri;
she is the sun, sharing
the horizon with the moon
who last night guarded the earth
and this morning passes on

Xaggu waa masniyo
Fooq iyo xaraar
Isha xiijiyoo;
Demesh iyo xariir
Ku xiddaysanoo
Cirka soo xansada.
Oo dad loo xil-qabo
Xamastoodu taal.

Togag baa dhex xula;
Biyii Xaramka iyo
Wiski xooriyaa
Dhex xumbaynayaan.

Xaggu waa dar-xumo;
Xaawaleey carruur
Ku xansheeran oo,
Xiiq iyo harraad
Xuurteeysan iyo
Xammaal iyo wastaad.

Afartaasi xidhan.

Xaggan kalena eeg:
Gabadheenna Xiis
Waa xabag-barsheed;
Waa xero-u-dhalan
Xulad geenyo ugub.
Oon xiito guluf
Dirir iyo xabbaadh
Loo sudhin xakame.

Waa xuural-cayn;
Iyo Xaaliyeey
Dayax xoosh ahoo
Xalay gaadh ahaa,
Saakana xarrago

his watch, elegantly
drawing back the hem,
the membrane of the sky
like closed curtains.

He paints the dawn sky
as she rises in her urgency
with the fletches on the arrows
of the morning's rays.

And she, in this flirtation,
because of his caresses,
these delicate advances,
lets herself be roused.

In her fever and her heat,
her rising and ripping,
self-consuming passion,
she throws off her clouds
and stands, the length of a forearm
from the horizon. Can you see
her whip-lithe limbs?
If I've failed
then ask her to forgive me.

* * *

Dearly-missed, our Xiis
was a navel to the river
of the people; she was part of them,
but penned in scrubland,
and fenced in the pen,
she did not have to see
that season which sears the trees,
feel its harshness or its heat.

Only once did she break out
only once feel the freedom

Xil-wareejintii,
Xuubkii cirkiyo
Daahyadi xidhnaa
Kor u xaydayoo;

Sagal xaradhyo lihi
Qorrax xiiso wado,
Xaraaraha bulka leh
Ku xiddeeyeyoo;

Xod-xodtooy iyana
Xaradhaamadiyo
Hab-xiloodintii
Xadantootayoo;

Xummad iyo kulayl
Naf-xaraare baas,
Xaam-xaamadkii
Xayn furatay oo
Xusul joogga le'eg.
Xaashaa kallaa!
Xubno-jeedalleey
Haddii aan xistiyey
"Xaal qaado" dhaha.

                    * * *

Gabadheenna Xiis
Xubin bay ahayd
Xuddun webi ku taal;
Oo xidh oodan iyo
Xakab loo dugsiyo;
Oon xagaaga arag
Dhirta xaalufshiyo
Xanaf iyo kulayl.

Mar uun bay 'xaf' tidhi;
Mar uun bay Xorriyo

of transgressing their strictures.
It was said of Eve that she
cut the rope that bound her,
breached her limits.

And so she tore the silk off
that used to cover the hole
in which the rat eats
afterbirth and blood clots,
deliberately exposing
its shameful weaknesses,
its irresponsibilities:
she set them out one by one.

That tree, the twigs
and dry branches of which were kindling,
the dead leaves a fuel
which used to threaten fire,
she confirmed to the people
as hollow, a tree
of poisonous resin.

She disclosed our strongest feelings,
that intense intimacy of love,
which enters into us all;
she longed for her elegant boy
who swept her away;
by not closing off
her clean desires,
she refused stability.

She didn't consider how,
betrothed through obligation,
she was another man's wife;
nor took into account
that place she came from,

Ka kufriday xumii;
Laye Xaawo hee!
Xadhka-gooysayaa;
Xadki jabisayaa.

Is-xabaal wax badan
Godka uu xabkiyo
Xinjiraha ku cuno,
Huwin jirey xariir
Ka xayuubisaa;
Xin u qaawisaa;
Ceebaha xilka leh
Xabbad-qaaddayaa.

Geedkii xaskiyo
Xuladada wax guba
Xaabuu u yahay
Loogu xeeban jirey,
Inu xabag-dhunkaal
Xordan yahay dadkii
U xaqiijisaa.

Xubbi iyo kalgacal
Laab xuunsho galay
La xariidisaa;
Dareenkeeda xalan
Iyadoon xidh-xidhin,
Hanadkii xasladay
Xiiseeysayaa;
Xasil diiddayaa.

Xusbaddana ma gelin
Inay xilo nin tahay
Qasab loogu xidhay;
Xaaleeyna-mayn
Xaafaddeey ka timi,

nor, poor girl,
the law that holds sway there.

* * *

As this liaison continued
it went beyond whispers.
As soon as the secret was out
the family of that princess,
those wrong-doers,
grew wrathful;
that gluttonous House
got angry.

That gifted girl
was found guilty of what?
Love that was tethered to
'the branch with short roots
that can't reach the heights;
the wild choice
of the wrong ram' –
so they threw her in jail.

Then, although no-one tried her,
that Holy Place of love
which was a seat for
her clean heart,
that shrine to passion
was opened by a bullet.

This is how it was told:
she and the boy she loved
were cut down
and put in their graves.

If you only remember one thing
about this story, let it be this:

Iyo Xaaliyeey
Xeerkii ka jirey.

* * *

Waxay xawlisaba
Xanti durugtayaa;
Xogsigii horeba
Xigtadii Gobaad,
Dir-xumaan-ku-nool
Ka xanaaqdayaa;
Baha-xaydho-weyn
Xayraantayaa.

Gabadhii Xaddiyo
Caashaqa ku xidhay
"Laan-gaabka xune
Xagga sare ahayn,
Xulashada gurracan
Ee sumal-xadka ah"
Ku xujoowdayaa;
Xabsi loo diryaa.

Iyadoon Xorriyo
Aan cidi xukumin
Qalbigii xallaa,
Xaramkii cishqiga
Xadradoow ahaa,
Taalladi xubbiga
Xabbad lagu furyaa.

Laye Xaadsan iyo
Xuurkeey jeclayd
Loogu xiiryeyaa;
La xabaalyeyaa.

Halna waa xusuus
Sheekada ku xidho:

the place is Hijaz,
the centre of the divine revelation,
destination of the hajj;
it is the navel of the Prophet,
where the Beloved of God was born.

Meeshu waa Xijaas
Xaruntii waxyiga
Halka loo xaj tago,
Ee Xabiibalaah
Xudduntiisu tahay.

SELF-MISUNDERSTOOD

Maxamed Xaashi Dhamac 'Gaarriye'

The literal translation of this poem was made by Martin Orwin. The
final translated version of the poem is by W N Herbert.

I can't understand you, curious self,
nor grasp how you're both life and death,
grabbed land and peaceful settlement,
grudging milker that makes me full,
sun set at evening whilst casting
noon's shortest shadow: how can you be
two who can't marry
yet share the same house?

How can I set this riddle and
give away its answer if
I fail to understand your secret
or even what you mean by it?

Are you something separate,
a stand-alone that leans
upon no man's shoulder,
or such a part of the people
that you can't be parted from them?

And are you that which is Gaarriye
or two opposing halves
he cannot fit together?
I call you, crooked creation:
bear witness to your character.

I can't get to grips with you, gregarious self
are you the same age as Gurey

GARAAD-DARAN

Maxamed Xaashi Dhamac 'Gaarriye'

Garaad-daran naftaydaay!
Geeri iyo nololeey!
Guluf lagu negaadaay!
Gabno laga dhergaayeey!
Gabbal dumay habeenoo,
Hadh gadiidan yahayeey!
Lammaan aan is-geyinoo,
Guri qudh ah u hooydaay!

Googgaada xaajada,
Gaaxdeedu waxay tahay,
Maan garan xogtaadee,
Maxaad uga gol leedahay?

Ma wax gaar ah baad t'oo
Goonidiisa jira oo,
Garab aan u baahnayn?
Mise gobol dadweynaha,
Ka go'aynnin baad tahay?

Maadigaa ah Gaarriye?
Mise laba gudboonoo,
Is-geleynin baad tiin?
Gurrac-loo-abuuryeey,
Bal geddaada ii sheeg.

Garaad-daran naftaydaay!
Gurey iyo cadceedaha,

and his fellow constellations?
Are you all kin?
And what about the history of the Greeks,
the Pharaoh's army and
the goring of kings,
what about the groans of war,
the dynasties you saw destroyed?
Bear witness to it all.

My limbs and all their molecules,
call them to the stand:
line them up in ranks,
collect their statements;
those million monsoons that marched past,
tell them to complete
the tale of that trek
which each one took, the night-walking
and the assignations,
where they were each afternoon
when they made Gaariye:
make their stories flow like milk.

I can't seem to fix you, quarrelsome self,
you're like that riverbed, Waaheen,
shifting between long drought, brief spate –
that business you concluded yesterday,
signed, sealed and celebrated,
today you snatch it back
and poke it full of holes.
Did you tear up all natal traits,
redraft infancy and all its rites?
Or did truth grow old, and find
its essence not eternal after all?
Where does the failure lie?
Your usual impact is to put
the people in two minds,

Isku gedo miyaad tiin?
Gacal miyaad wadaagtaan?

Bal Giriig warkiisiyo
Guutadii Fircoon iyo
Waxa boqor la gawracay,
Ama aad gariir iyo
Guri ba'ay u taagnayd,
Googoos u mariyoo;
Giddi waaxyahaygiyo,
U galaydh xubnaha oo;
Midba gees u taagoo,
Ka gur sheekadoodoo;
Malaayiin gu' oo tegey
Ku dheh gebaggebeeyoo;
Geeddigoodi dheeraa,
Mid kastaa guduudiga,
Halkay galabba joogtiyo,
Goorteey kulmeenee,
Gaarriye sameeyeen,
Godolkeeda ii mari.

Garaad-daran naftaydaay!
Sida gacanka Waaheen
Hadba gaaf-wareegaay!
Arrin aad gorfeysiyo
Waxaad shalay u guuxdaad,
Maantana ka giigtaa
Gol-daloolo yeeshee;
Miyaad dhalan-geddoontoo
Dib bay kuu gardaadsheen?
Ma runtaa gaboowdoo
Geedkeedu waareyn?
Guul-darradu dhankay tahay?

Guud ahaan waxaad tahay
Dadku kugu go'doonyoo

to keep them from deciding:
one casts you as the hero
they could never see back down;
while another thinks you short of wits –
your way lost, your well dry –
a barren camel; another one
misses you as he'd miss his own son –
if a speck of grit scratched you
he could not be consoled;
one casts you as cobra,
trustless as a looter; while another
has you as the strong shoulder,
a sure repayer of kindness,
deserving of good deeds,
a shelter and a shield.

Unquantified soul, secret from yourself,
ungraspable for others –
they all fall short in the fathoming.
Did anyone ever track you down
and shake you by the hand
or did they all end up lost?
Or could it be you who fails them?
Hiding within your shapeshifting,
a different colour for each place,
each night a new beast, a different face?

I can't get to grips with this garrulous self
even if my lope outstrips
the galloping of ostriches or horses,
even if I vanish from their horizons,
enter and depart from orbit
in the same instant you are with me,
you never fall short of my side.
Wherever I stand, whenever I stop,
you stand and stop with me

Isla waa go'aanoo,
Mid baad geesi adagoo
Gabbanayn la tahayoo;
Maan-gaab lumaayiyo
Mid baa ceel ganuuniyo
Kuu haysta gocoroo;
Mid baa kugu goblama oo
Gurxankiisu damihayn
Haddii saxar ku gaadhoo;
Gaadaa wax boobiyo
Mid baad good la tahayoo;
Mid baad garab laxaadliyo
Ruux guda abaaloo,
Loo galo wanaag iyo
Gaashaan la tahayoo;

Garaadlaay xogtaadii,
Cidi gaadhi waydee,
Dadkan kugu gabaabsiyey,
Kumaa helay guntaadoo
Gacan-qaad la siiyaa?
Miyey gabi habaabeen?
Maadigaa wax gabayoo,
Hadba geed is-mariyoo,
Goobba midab la joogoo,
Gallibaxa habeenkii?

Garaad-daran naftaydaay!
In kastoon gucleeyoo,
Garmaamada haldhaagiyo
Gammaankaba ka jiitoo,
Cirka sare galaa-baxo,
Adigay la gooshoo,

Iga gaabinaynoo,
Goobtaan is-taagaba,

as though I carried round a debt
and someone said, 'Collect it!'
as though you were a good catch,
a woman looking for a husband.
Why is it you never sleep,
following me everywhere?

Whatever crime I commit,
whatever ugliness I enter into;
each shameful deed
that is my very own –
even though I gird myself to lie,
pull on another mask
to leave people at a loss –
you record each defect
as though set down on tape,
insidiously fill me with guilt,
obligation, injury:
you see through me as a wife does –
but why understand me by my flaws?

Curious, gregarious, garrulous self,
did you fail to grasp the stifling norms?
To quarrel with those who rap our knuckles
for whom only their diktats
need be acknowledged,
and not what you conclude:

You don't deserve the problems
that barrack and assail you.
Remember the marriage ceremony
of your father and weep;
bewail your mother because of
the afternoon you entered her womb
and the world, blame her.

Adigaa galluubane,
Ma gashaygu baaqdoo,
Lagu yidhi ka soo goo?
Mise gaari inan oo,
Guur-u-meer ah baad tahay?
Maxaad gama' u diiddee,
Iga daba-gureysaa?

Dambiyaal waxaan galo,
Ama geysto fool-xumo,
Gabigoodba ceebaha,
Aan gaar u leeyahay;
In kastoon is-giijoo,
Weji kale gashada oo,
Dadka been ku gaasiro,
Adigaa giraanoo,
Gunta iimahaygoo,
Hoos ii guhaadshee;
Godobtiyo xumaantada,
Inaad tahay ninkeed-gaba,
Maxaad iigu garataa?

Garaad-daran naftaydaay!
Gumaysaad ku nooshoo,
Dadkaa kugu garaacdoo,
Guddoonkooda mooyee,
Kaa gareysan maayaan,
Waxad adigu goysee;
Maad galabsan hawlaha
Kugu gaardiyaayee,
Galbiskii adoogaa,
Goco oo ilmeeyoo,
Hooyadaa u goohoo,
Galabtay ku dihatiyo,
Eerso uur-galkaagii.

I HAVE BECOME AN APOSTATE OF LOVE

Maxamed Xaashi Dhamac 'Gaarriye'

The translation of this poem was made by Rhoda A Raghe and was published on redsea-online.com in 2006.

Desire, go in vain.
Fragile levee bend.
Broken promise, heed my argument.
Deception, kneel down.
False clouds evaporate.
Love, diminish.
Receding sea waters move.
Let the fallen branch thud.
Cupid, withdraw your arrows.
Bats and flying birds come.
Sing chorally with me.
Worshipers of full pockets,
Wrap Faith for them.
Humble, hear my argument.
I landed on the place you marked.
I am a constantly flowing spring.
The albatross I hang on your neck,
Will block you from every entrance.
Your double faced love,
Your lack of consistency,
Your conspiracies to sabotage,
Your chameleon attitude,
Will catch up with you.
If you suffer punches on the way,
Don't turn back to me.
I am an apostate of love.

KA KUFRIYEY JACAYLKII (1978)

Maxamed Xaashi Dhamac 'Gaarriye'

Jamashooy waxba ha tarin;
Jarka debecsanaw ciir;
Ballankii jabaw dood;
Beeneey jilbaha dhigo.

Jirka gaagaxaw baga;
Dihmo uur-jilaycaw.

Badda jiidaneey guur;
Jibintii dhacdaay yeedh;
Dib u guro cir-jiidhkaw.

Fiintiyo jugleydaay,
Ila jiibsha heesaha;
Dadka jeebka caabuda,
U jaxaasa iimaan.

Han-yareey jawaab hoo;
Shaxdaad jeexday waan degay;
Irmaan baanay joogtaa;
Jaraan guudka kuu sudhay;
Jid kastaana kaa xidhan.

Laba-geel-jeclaantii,
Hadba-doc-u-janjeedhkii,
Jillaafooyinkaagiyo,
Jirjirroolenimadii,
Jaasadeeda waad heli.

Last night's confusion,
The short nap I had,
Did I live in a bad dream?
The heaven I wished for,
When the flesh woke up,
Did woe bid farewell?
The sustenance I anticipated,
The seclusion I planned for,
When did the neighbours moved in?
The ill I wanted to heal,
The house I wanted to build,
The boulder I wanted to cross,
The interest I wanted to protect,
My planned forecast
I was supposed to achieve,
I was leading a Jinn's mirage!
The trunk I planted,
I made the canal for,
My personal strife,
That was to be nurtured with songs
Was covered with termites.
Except for the callous skin,
There was no stalk inside.
How varied are dreams!
How misleading is a mirage!
How internal suffering
Is difficult for insomnia!
I wish I had stayed put!

Hadday jugo ku gaadhaan,
Waxba hay jadeer-wicin,
Ka kufriyey jacayjkii.

Xalay jaha-wareerkii,
Hurdadaan yar jiifsaday,
Riyo jaan miyaan galay.?

Jannadaan ladaabsaday,
Kolkii jiidhku oogsaday,
Jab miyaa sagootiyey?

Jabadkaan astaystiyo,
Jeeskaan yagleelsaday,
Hadmaa jaarku i ag dagay?

Jirradaan bogsiin laa,
Gurigaan "jiq" siin laa,
Garbadaan lahaa jiidh,
Dantaydaan lahaa jiri,
Jaan-gooyadaydaan
Is-lahaa ka jibo-keen,
Shaw dhaan jin baan waday!

Jirriddaan tallaalee,
U soo jeexay laagtee,
Jeedaaladaydiyo,
Jiiftada ku korin laa,
Xar baa shaw ku jeerraa!
Dusha jidhifta mooyee,
Shaw dhuuxba kuma jirin!

Riyo jaadad badanaa!
Dhalanteed jimcoonaa!
Uur-jireenka murugada
Soo-jeed u daranaa!
Iska jiif lahaydaa!

WATERGATE

Maxamed Xaashi Dhamac 'Gaarriye'

This poem was composed in 1976 after the United States used its veto in
the UN Security Council against the entry of the newly independent
state of Angola under Neto. The translation of this poem was made by
Rhoda A Rageh and was published on redsea-online.com in March 2006.

Oh Carter, Suspicion overwhelms my sense of alliance.
What I learn from the leaves in volumes of experience,
Humanity still groans from the perils you caused.
To pose some questions baffling my mind, May I ask
Who afflicted the brotherhood I honored?
Who, in his prejudice played the double-faced?
Danger looms for he, who herds a strayed flock.
Like a woman in black for the death of a husband,
By God, I was aggrieved by the death of Malcolm X.
Who is the hyena that devoured the awakened warrior?
When a hero stirs enraged who force-feed him with bitterness?
Who marshaled the men that cut Martin Luther King's throat?
The Red Indians - who ruined to reduce their numbers?
By God, the blows you preside are inconceivable.
Nixon's shame pales in contrast to the infamy in your records.
I bet Watergates are more than you are letting us in.

Palestine's woe withers the truth-knower with gloom.
When their land was seized despoiled and desecrated.
They are left wanderers forever into foreign lands.
They enter not a hut, nor a shed to hide from severe winters.
On that homeless society, who compelled them to be?
Are there no partners with Jews on their laurels of shame?
By God, the blows you preside are inconceivable.

WOOTARGAYT

Maxamed Xaashi Dhamac 'Gaarriye'

Wiswis bayga galay Kaartarow weheshigiinniiye,
Waayo-arag intii aan ka helay buugaggii weriyey
Wareerkaad baddeen buu khalqigu weli la taahaaye,
Su'aalaan ku weydiinayaa ila sal waaweyne,
Walaalnimadii aan koolin jirey waadhka yaa geliyey?
Isagoo takoor wada ayaa laba wejiileeyey?
Waadaasha xoolaha lumaa weere waw halise,
Hadba weerka naag baw xidhaan weydey kii qabaye,
Wedkii Maalkom Ekis waan ka naxay wacad Ilaahaye,
Waa kee waraabaha dharqaday warangalkii toosay?
Kolka geesi weyraxo ayaa dacar waraabsiiyey?
Yaa wadey raggii Luudar Kiin waagi hanaq gooyey?
Hindidii casayd yaa waddarey wadarna yaw laayey?

Alla weger waxaad belo dhigteen waa ka waasacane,
Niksan way la sahal ceeb haddaad ka welwelaysaane,
Qirta Wootargaytyadu ka badan taydun weriseene!

Walbahaarka Falasdiin nin ogi qulub la weydowye,
Waddankoodi goortii la dhacay wahabku kooreeye,
Waa debed-wareeggii sidii woohow loo yidhiye,
Waab iyo ardaa kama galaan weedhka karameede,
Ummaddaasi wadhan yaa sidaa waajib kaga yeelay?
Miyaan lala wadaagayn Yuhuud wiirsigiyo ceebta?

Nixon's shame pales in contrast to the infamy in your records.
I bet Watergates are more than you are letting us in.
What you subjected to Vietnam stunned all human races.
At dawn, the downpour of your heaviest weapons,
Planes maneuvering over a morning in confusion
Shells like raindrops, the hue of flying bullets,
An informed adult remembers Saigon in distress;
When the jeering wilder beast feasting on baby parts and,
The piteous howl of wailing mothers echoed one another.
As I still sob for the men you speared,
My Memory will not efface the sight of the oldest man.
Of weeping for Ho Chi Min, my eyelids have run dry.
By God, the blows you preside are inconceivable.
Nixon's shame pales in contrast to the infamy in your records
I bet Watergates are more than you are letting us in.
The Woobis of Angola and the ensued confusion
To stop the devastation of harmful Portugal,
When they reached their limit and mounted their horses;
With their long struggle when the flag finally emerged, and
Thunderous downpours ripped open all river banks.
After onset blessings and Neeto Whidif sought
His seat in the United Nations; I cannot
Comprehend what ailed that lawful demand.
Strange! Why did your VETO wring their right?
By God, the blows you preside are inconceivable.
Nixon's shame pales in contrast to the infamy in your records.
I bet Watergates are more than you are letting us in.
Like a salty well you discarded us after you'd your fill
Your industries are watered with the blood I spit.
Foolish is he who embarks with the hypocrite.
I outgrew believing oaths packaged with glittering lies.
I carry Zimbabwe's plight, lonesome, like a desert flower.
Some men are still cut off from the Namibian River.
Lacking your guidance Ian Smith could not throw slingshots.
By God, the blows you preside are inconceivable.

Alla weger waxaad belo dhigteen waa ka waasacane,
Niksan wayla sahal ceeb haddaad ka welwelaysaane,
Qirta Wootargaytyadu ka badan taydun weriseene!

Fiyatnaam wixii aad baddeen uunku wada yaabye,
Hubka waarriyuun baad aroor wagac ku siiseene,
Dayuurado waleecaad qabaa geliyey weesaaqe,
Sida dhibic wajiineed wixii gumuc is-weydaartey,
Nin waraystay waa garanayaa wahankii Saygoone,
Goortuu wasaashaday dhurwaa waaxyihii ubadka,
Isu baxe wishiiriga ci'diyo wiida naaguhuye,
Raggaad waranka siiseen anoo weli u ooyaaya,
Marna waxaan i deynayn duqii ugu fil weynaaye,
Weheey! geeridii Hoo Shi Miin wiilashay gudhaye.

Alla weger waxaad belo dhigteen waa ka waasacane,
Niksan wayla sahal ceeb haddaad ka welwelaysaane,
Qirta Wootargaytyadu ka badan taydun weriseene!

Woobiga Angoolee qarxaday wiriirigtii yeedhay,
Boortuqiiskii wiiqay rabeen inay ku waabshaane,
Goortuu wadnaha taabtay bay wegen u fuuleene,
Waxay waarrisaba maalintuu calanku waaheelmay,
Waqalkiyo daruurihii onkoday webiyadii dooxmay,
Guushii kolkii loo waqlalay Neeto widhif raadshey,
In wakiil u tago *Yuu-En-Oo* golaha waaheelan,
Maan garan halkuu weyd ka yahay waajibkaa cadiye,
Wadhiyey! Maxaad ugu riddeen walagta fiitooda?

Alla weger waxaad belo dhigteen waa ka waasacane,
Niksan wayla sahal ceeb haddaad ka welwelaysaane,
Qirta Wootargaytyadu ka badan taydun weriseene!

Sida ceel wiyeeraad kol hore nooga wabaxdeene,
Warshaddiinna dhiiggaan tufaa lagu waraabshaaye,
Garaad ma laha ruuxii wabiin wacad la qaataaye,

Nixon's shame pales in contrast to the infamy in your records.
I bet Watergates are more than you are letting us in.

Ka il baxay wallaahida afkaa walalac beenaade,
Werwerkii Simbaab waan qabaa Weris-la-mooddiiye,
Waadiga Namiibiya rag baa waayir xidhayaaye,
Idinkaa watee Yaan Ismiidh wadhaf ma tuureene.

Alla weger waxaad belo dhigteen waa ka waasacane,
Niksan wayla sahal ceeb haddaad ka welwelaysaane,
Qirta Wootargaytyadu ka badan taydun weriseene!

KUDU

Maxamed Xaashi Dhamac 'Gaarriye'

This poem was composed by Gaarriye in 1980 and is a political
allegory. The kudu is a species of antelope. It is a large animal and
the male has long twisting horns. The literal translation of this poem
was made by Martin Orwin and Maxamed Xasan 'Alto'. The final
translated version of the poem is by David Harsent.

My father told me this story
when I was a child. We sat
in the shade of a tree and he began:
Long ago there lived a king
who sprouted a pair of horns - just buds,
at first, but he checked them every day
and wore his turban low to hide
this blemish, to hide this mark of shame.
But a king, of course, doesn't wash his own hair!
His man-servant knew all about the king's shame
and day by day the knowledge grew
inside him, a word that had to be spoken,
a terrible secret that had to be told.
They said, You're mistaken.
He said, No.
They said, Dead men keep secrets.
He said, Ah...
There were people, he knew, who would feed on such news,
but his daily bread stuck in his throat.
There were people, he knew, who dreamed of such news,
but he slept on a bed of burning coals.

Then, one night, he could bear it no longer.
He left his house, he walked out of the village,

MADAX GOODIR

Maxamed Xaashi Dhamac 'Gaarriye'

Mar aan gaban ahaa beri
Galab aan adoogay
Geed uu fadhiyi jirey
Sheeko kooban kaga guray,
Wuxuu yidhi: "guyaal hore
Boqor geesalaa jirey
Oo goostay weligii
Inaan iinta lagu garan.

Fule waa geddiisee,
Wuxuu goorba hubiyoo
Gedfo oo cimaamado,
Nin gaadhaa sirtii helay
Godob buuse taransaday
Garashadu u sabab tahay
Qof gafaana laga dhigay,
Hadduu gaabsan waayana
Inuu gowrac jiro maqal.

Hadba giirka loo kici
Goldalooladuu helay
Inay gudubto loo diid.

Isna waa gartiisee,
Liqi waa gasiinkii;

mile after mile in a torrent of darkness
and came to the watering holes, where the eagle
took flight at his footstep, where the gentle gazelle
shied and ran. He sat by the water
and thought, 'There was a time when such things
could be openly said. Yes, there was a time
when even the poor could be told the truth.'
When dawn-light shone through the trees, he dug
with his hands, deep down, as a beast digs a den
and placed his mouth close to the hole
he'd made and whispered his terrible secret
to the earth: 'King Goojaa, King Goojaa has horns.
Horns like the kudu. The king has horns!'
Don't interrupt, my father said.
Please don't ask me what these things mean.
It's just a story I got from my father,
And he from his. Do you want to know
how it ends? Then listen: when the man told his tale
to the earth, the burden left him, it went
underground, and the man, why, he brushed himself down
and went on his way. And this is the strangest
part of the story: that even today,
when the soft rain falls on that place in the bush,
that very same place where he planted his secret,
horns like the kudu's grow from the ground.

War guntamay la foolqaad,
Hadba gaadhka meel dhigay
Dadka uurka googo'ay
sida garac ka wada qari,
Kuna oloshey gogoshii."

"Goobyaalka laylkii.
Kolkay gama' is waayeen
Gelin dhexe rugtiisiyo
Gurigii ka soo bood,
Gudcur beegsey duurkiyo
Geliyada dugaagga leh
Mugdigii galaydhkiyo
Garanuugta kala didi,
Gocoshiyo xasuus iyo
Kalgacayl sabooleed
Gaashaan ka sii dhigay."

"Wuxuu gebidhacleeyaba,
Kolkii waagu galac yidhi,
Geed hoostii faadhfaadh,
Sidii bahal god dheer qoday,
Dabadeed gafuurkiyo
Gadhka ciidda saaryoo
La faq goofkii keligii,
Dulucdiina gaadhsii,
'Inuu boqorka Goojaa
Madax goodir leeyahay'."

Hadda iga ma goyside
Waxaad iga guraysaa,
Sheeko beri la ii galay.

"Geesigii warkiisii,
Kii cabudhay kolkii ganay,
Garbihiisa laga duul,
Gebigii fudayd noqoy,

Goobtiina aasyoo,
Ka hurgufay go'iisii,
Galbay oo ka sii socoy."
"Ka gadaalna meeshii
Laye 'goortii roob helay,
Geesaa ka soo baxay.'"

ARROGANCE

Maxamed Xaashi Dhamac 'Gaarriye'

The literal translation of this poem was made by Martin Orwin. The final translated version of the poem is by W N Herbert.

Wandered brood of Adam,
lost, bewildered people,
hear what I have to say.

Stop for a moment before the mountains
and for the simple sake of awe
be humbled, let your tears fall.

Look to, look through the air above,
be moved by the sight of stars,
watch their bodies wheel.

Ask the thunder, see what lightning says,
the rain-bearing wind which blows
the good grey cloud, ask them.

The camel's old keen for her calf,
be hushed and hear it, hear how
the birds' song weeps with it: weep with them too.

How the sea sounds out its old chorus,
what moves in its abyssal womb:
acknowledge these and what they mean.

Examine the earth at your feet,
the rush of the rivers,
raise your eyes to the clouds.

AADMI

Maxamed Xaashi Dhamac 'Gaarriye'

Aadmiyahaw hallaysani!
Ambadyahaw wareersani!
Maqal ereyadaydoo,
Buuraha ag joogsoo,
Amakaag daraaddii,
Ilmo gabax ka siiyoo,
Cirka sare u eegoo,
Xiddiggaha astaysoo,
Arag felegga meeroo,
Onkodkiyo hillaaciyo,
Ufadaa dhacaysiyo
Uurada waraysoo,
Ololkeeda Gooraan.

Aammus oo dhegeysoo,
Shimbiraha la ooyoo,
Badda "aw"-da haysiyo
Waxa uurka ugu jira,
Axadhoo garwaaqsoo.
Dhulka aad u baadhoo,
Webiyada ordaayiyo
Daruuraha indheeyiyo,
Oogada jalleecoo,
Ciirada aroortiyo,
Dabaylaha af garo oo,
Uduggooda kaymaha,

Glimpse what lies above
the auroral mist, the winds,
understand what these things have to say.

The scent of wild acacia -
inhale it, relish it, and
delight in the green of pastures.

Count up the lineage of all life,
mark the endless days and days:
this worthless arrogance of yours,
you have to let it go.

All nebulae and galaxies,
the Camel of the Southern Cross,
our own burning sun, who said these
were lit for humankind?

Before a man was made in this world
didn't Virgo blaze above?
Aren't all those gatherings of stars
far older than us?
Since when was their high light
kindled only for you?

Exactly when do you think the heavens
were told to carry out the order
'Confine yourselves to the human race'?
If you simply ceased to be
wouldn't their light continue?
Wouldn't it be then as it is now?

Wandered brood of Adam,
your bluster is a lie.
You shared this womb with all
wild things that roam,

Urso oo jeclaysoo,
Ku ilwaadso dooggoo,
U abtiri naflaydoo,
Ayaamaha tilmaansoo,
Aabiga bilaashka ah,
Waa inaad illowdaa.

Afaggaalayaashiyo,
Cadceeddeenna oloshiyo,
Awrka samada yaa yidhi,
Aadmigay u shidanyiin?

Ifkoon cidi ku uunnayn,
Miyaan Dirirku oognayn?

Ururradu miyaanay,
Kaa ayni weynayn?
Ilayskooda goormaa,
Loo daaray awgaa?

Hadmaa felegga oosha ah,
Amar buuxa lagu yidhi,
Ku ekaw dadkoo qudha?

Haddaad eegga madhataan,
Miyaanuu iftiimayn,
Sidiisaa ahaanayn?

Aadmiyahaw hallaysani,
Amarkaagu waa been,
Waxaad uur wadaagtaan,
Ugaadhaa wareegtoo,
Ugbaadkiyo caleentaad,
Uur wada gasheenoo,
Uumiyaha dhammaantii,
Ilmaadeer gudboon iyo

all roots that flourish,
you entered this world together.

All creation is your cousin,
each creature your equal
and you share an ancestor:
all living things are to you
as stick is to bark, bark to stick.
You and they are like two eyes -
when one sheds tears
the other weeps.
They were not made for you alone,
nor were they created to serve.

Of everything which is, half is secret -
however things appear
the meaning is always deeper.

Isir baad tihiinoo;
Noolahaad arkaysaa,
Waa ul iyo diirkeed;
Waa sida indhaha oo,
Kolkay midi ilmaysaa,
Ta kaleeto ooydaa.

Looma uumin keligaa
Inay kuu adeegaan.

Ammuuraha badh baa sir ah;
Sida xaal u eg yahay,
Ujeeddadu ka xeeldheer.

A-Z

Maxamed Xaashi Dhamac 'Gaarriye'

The literal translation of this poem was made by Martin Orwin and
Mohamed Hasan "Alto". The final translated version of the poem is
by David Harsent.

Caalin, listen, I'm going to travel
From A to Z carried by language -
The alphabet, alive on the page.
I write the words and send them to you;
You sing to the wind and the crows as they fly
Carry my lines through the noonday sky
Chanting each to each. The ants
Become orators. The gossiping camels
Crowd the waterhole, eager for rumours.
Even the trees, as they rustle their leaves,
Are sharing a joke; the sheep and goats
Talk tough as they sniff out the latest news.
The hum of the breeze in the river-bed
Is the language of pride; the termites talk
With a tap and a touch; the clouds compose
Poems as only they can; the land
Speaks in prose of growth and gain
And the sound of rain in the season of rain
Rumbles like thunder and why this should be
Is something only the rain can explain.
I write these words and send them to you
To let you know that we live through language.
Without it - deformity, ugliness, illness;
Without it - no anchor for culture; without it
No making of maps, no naming of nations.
A man might boast of property, money,

TA'IYO WOW

Maxamed Xaashi Dhamac 'Gaarriye'

Caalinow, Ta' iyo Wow,
Bal tixraac halkaan maro!
Tukayaasha duulaa
Warka waysu tebiyaan;
Waa aftahan qudhaanjadu;
Geeluna tawaawaca
Kolka biyaha loo tubo
Ways tibaax yaqaannaa;
Tigaaddaad arkaysaa
Kaftan ay taqaannay
Hoos-ka-tuur u leedahay;
Taaha adhigu waa hadal
Urtu waysku toydaa;
Togaggiyo dabayluhu
Tookh bay la reemaan;
Tankiisuu aboorkuba
Toos ugu xidhiidhaa;
Daruuruhu tub gaaray,
Heesaha u tiriyaan;
Dhulku wuu tiraabaa,
Tifta roobka dayruhu,
Onkod buu la taamaa.

Waxay hoga-tusaysaa,
Afku nolosha waw tiir,
La'aantiisna tuur iyo

Position, but if he's unable to write
He's a pauper. Caalin, listen, your pen
Is your wealth, you're less than nothing without it.
Ask the old Gods how our culture has grown.
Think back to the time when our language suffered
One onslaught after the other: invasions,
Armies crossing our borders, the songs
Our fathers once sang destroyed or derided,
Our epics fading in memory, even
Our idioms gradually losing their meanings.
Every lost syllable tells in my heartbeat,
Every lost line is a scar on my heart.
Poems go hand-over-hand to create
A chain of wisdom, a chain that goes
From strength to strength; when this was shattered,
When our chain of poems was broken and scattered,
We were left with nothing but fragments, nothing
But scraps of wisdom - our inheritance
Nothing more than a handful of images.
Our story - a story so ancient that only
The Old Gods recall it - was gone forever.
Our children will never recover that wisdom:
Our legends and myths and the words of the prophets...
Remember the time when a man from the north
Wrote a letter received by a man from the south
And the second man threw the letter away,
Since the first man's language was foreign to him?
Remember the time when a camel was owned
By two men who needed to talk things through,
So a third man came in as interpreter?
Remember how politicians decided
To give us a written language? Remember
The fighting and feuding, the shouting and swearing?
Ten years went by with nothing decided
Until someone in power said, 'Latin!' and then
Somalia sat down and uncapped its pen.

Tulux lagama waayeen;
Tayo may lahaateen;
Dhaqan lama tallaaleen;
Qaran lama tusmaysteen;
Nin kastaa ha tookhee;
Far baa lagu tanaadaa.

Haddii qalinka loo tudho,
Wax qoraalka laga tago,
Lama taabbaggeli karo.

Waaq iyo Tinniix iyo
Bal Tincaaro weyddii,
Soo tiri ayaamaha,
Taariikhda raacdee.

Afkaygow, tabaaliyo
Maxaad tow ku nooleyd!
Maxaad belo u taagneyd!
Shisheeyuhu tab iyo xeel
Muxuu kugu tuntuunsaday,
Tisqaadkaaga dhaawacay!
Maxaa gabay tilmaannaa,
Maahmaaho toolmoon,
Maalmuhu tireenoo
Qalbigaygu tebayaa!
Maxaa erey tafiir go'ay!
Maxaan maanso teeriya,
Tacab ba'ay ka joogaa!
Sida ay u taxan tahay,
Murtidaadu tabanaa!
Teelteelna badanaa!

Maxaan sheeko taabud ah,
Tawraadi faallayn,
Weli nebina soo tebin,
Kaa tasoobay oo lumay!

I dreamed of that day! The pen and the page -
A poet's stock-in-trade. The choice
Finally made. The alphabet
Taking the first few steps of a journey
And never looking back. A new age
Of wisdom in poetry, yes, a new
Tradition! Go, now, and wake Sayid -
Give him the news, tell all the great
Poets our language lives again,
And this time written to last in lines
That can't be lost or thrown away.
Caalin, write lyrics, write epics, write verse
That beats in the brain and tells on the pulse;
Write poems of love, write poems that show
How myths can revive and language grow.
Enough! I've written all that I need
To write, except to praise the men
Who talked the language into being -
Statesmen, thinkers, poets, who gave
Somali poets a new way with words.
We could raise a statue to them and set it
Above the image of Jupiter...
Or perhaps we should honour them in poems
That use all the letters from A to Z.

Ubadkaagu toos iyo
Maxay talada seegeen!
Maxaa taar mid soo diray,
Ka kaleeto tuuroo,
Laba tulud wadaagtaa,
Turjubaan u baahdeen!

Qoraalkaagu tacab iyo
Muxuu dhigay turxaannoo,
Tartan ba'an aloosoo,
Colba doc iska taageen!

Allaylehe tabtaan rabay,
Haddaa lagu tixgeliyoo,
Tacluustiyo wadeecada,
Caawaba ka togatee,
Taw wiif ka siiyoo,
Taltallaabso maantoo,
Murtidaadu waa toge!
Taageer hiddaayoo,
Sayidkii ku toosoo,
Taabsii xogtaadoo,
Ku tirow Balaayacas!
Soo toosi Haabiil!
Raage taranta gaadhsii!

U tukubi higgaaddoo,
Soddon tirada dhaafsii!
Toban shaqal ku geeraar!
Shibbannaha ku taakuli!

Hadal lama tasoobee,
Guddigii ku tiirshee
Kugu taxay xuruufaha,
Mahad iyo tahniyad sii;
Taalladay mutaysteen,
Ka dultaag Cirjiidhyada.

BIOGRAPHIES

Martin Orwin

Martin Orwin was born in 1963. He studied Arabic and Amharic as an undergraduate at SOAS and he then went on to obtain a PhD in the phonology of Somali. Currently Senior Lecturer in Somali and Amharic at SOAS, he has taught there since 1992. He's published numerous articles on Somali language and poetry, and has carried out a good deal of pioneering research in the Horn of Africa. Martin has ongoing research interests in the metrics of Somali poetry and has translated a number of Somali poems, two of which were published in Modern Poetry in Translation (No.17 Mother Tongues Special Edition 2001). Martin has worked closely with a number of Somali poets including Gaarriye and Hadraawi and is a long-term supporter of the Poetry Translation Centre.

Abdirahman Farah 'Barwaaqo'

Abdirahman Farah 'Barwaaqo' is a linguist, poet, lexicographer, and an independent researcher. He is the author of several published books and numerous articles. "Magac bilaash uma baxo" ("No name is given without reason") is among his popular works and it is a pioneering work in the field of Somali Onomastics. He also compiled two dictionaries (Modern Somali-English dictionary and a dictionary of traditional medicine). He is the editor-in-chief of Hal-aqoon, a Journal of Somali Literature and Culture.

Maxamed Xasan 'Alto'

Maxamed Xasan 'Alto' was born in 1960. He studied in Mogadishu, Somalia, and Soviet Union and has an MA in Journalism. Since 2004 he has been a teacher in Somali language at SOAS London. He is a writer and freelance journalist and has published and edited many books in Somali language. He has worked closely with Martin Orwin on a number of Somali poetry translation and is closely involved with the Poetry Translation Centre.

David Harsent
David Harsent is Visiting Professor at Hallam University, Sheffield and a Fellow of the Royal Society of Literature. He has published nine volumes of poetry. Legion, won the Forward Prize for best collection 2005 and was shortlisted for both the Whitbread Award and the T.S. Eliot Prize. His Selected Poems (2007), was shortlisted for the Griffin International Poetry Prize. Night was published in January 2011. It was Poetry Book Society Choice for the Spring and was shortlisted for the T.S. Eliot Award, the Costa Poetry Prize and the Forward Prize.

W. N. Herbert
W. N. Herbert was born in Dundee in 1961. He is Professor of Poetry and Creative Writing at Newcastle University, and publishes mostly with Bloodaxe Books. His translations (with Martin Orwin) of Gaarriye appeared from Enitharmon in 2008. He is grateful to the Poetry Translation Centre for all their support.

Sarah Maguire
Sarah Maguire was born in West London in 1957. She is a poet and translator whose poetry was first published in 1989 in the series New Chatto Poets. Sarah is the founder and director of the Poetry Translation Centre, which opened in 2004. The PTC emerged from the poetry translation workshops she inaugurated whilst she was the Royal Literary Fund Writing Fellow at the School of Oriental and African Studies at the University of London (2001-2003). Through its unique pairings of leading British poets with linguists, the PTC has translated poets from South Korea to Somaliland.

Poetry Translation Centre
The Poetry Translation Centre was established by the poet Sarah Maguire in 2004 to translate contemporary poetry from Africa, Asia and Latin America to a high literary standard. Poetry thrives on

translation: it's impossible to imagine English poetry without it. From Chaucer, via Wyatt, Dryden and Pope, to Ezra Pound's Cathay, translation has been its life-blood. But English poetry has yet to engage with the rich poetic traditions of the many languages now spoken in the UK; for Islamic communities in particular, poetry is a particularly significant art form. PTC work aims to redress that deficiency. By making their poetry at home in English, PTC aims to celebrate the cultures of communities that are frequently neglected and abused in the UK, inviting them to play a vital role in British cultural life. See www.poetrytranslationcenter.org.

Kayd Somali Arts and Culture
Kayd Somali Arts and Culture is an organization based in London and is promoting Somali culture, literature and arts. Kayd's aim is to contribute to the creation of the concept of tolerance and an appreciation of the diversity of Somali cultures through education, promoting writing, reading, performances, festivals, debates and discussions like the Somali Week Festival which takes place in October every year as integral part of the Black History Month activities in London. See www.kayd.org.

Redsea-Online Cultural Foundation
Redsea-Online is based in Italy and in Somaliland and promotes the culture of reading and creative writing in Somali speaking societies, with particular focus on youth. Redsea Foundation also supports and promotes Information and Communication Technology for development within the Somaliland society. It promotes and distributes proven quality Somali literature contents (essays, history, fiction, science, poetry and drama); provides young people with access to the cultures of the world by translating international renowned classical literature (including fiction, poetry and drama) into Somali; and yearly organizes Hargeysa International Book Fair, the main cultural event and book celebration in Somaliland. Redsea Foundation's main target is to value and to preserve Somali traditional human-created wisdom (literature, indigenous science, traditional games, language and all other forms of art of human expression) in the form of the written word. See www.redsea-online.com

FURTHER READING

Cabdiraxmaan C. Faarax "Barwaaqo", *Mahadhada Iyo Waxqabadka Maxamed Xaashi Dhamac "Gaarriye"*, 2007, Hal-Aqoon Publishers, Calgary.

Maxamed Xaashi Dhamac "Gaarriye", *poems / maansooyin*, 2008, Translated by W. N. Herbert and Martin Orwin, Enitharmon Press, London.

Maxamed Xaashi Dhamac "Gaarriye", *Toddobaadka iyo suugaanta*, 1967, A weekly series of articles on literature: 9 articles (24,31 January; 7,14 February; 27 March; 3,8,29 May), Xiddigta Oktoober, Muqdisho.

Maxamed Ibraahin Warsame "Hadraawi", Siciid Saalax Axmed, Maxamed Xaashi Dhamac "Gaarriye", Muuse Cabdi Climi, *Aqoon iyo Afgarad*, 1972, Wasaaradda Waxbarashada iyo Barbaarinta, Muqdisho.

Martin Orwin, *On the concept of 'definitive text' in Somali poetry*, 2003, Bulletin of SOAS, 66, 3 (2003), 334–347.

Martin Orwin, Maxamed Xasan "Alto" & Yaasiin Jaamac Nuux "Suldaan" (eds), *Hagarlaawe*, 2007. Diiwaanka Maansooyinka Maxamed Xaashi Dhamac "Gaarriye", Aftahan Publications, London.

PTC, 2012, Poetry Translation Center website: accessed on 16/08/2012 www.poetrytranslation.org/poets/Maxamed_Xaashi_Dhamac_'Gaarriye'

RSOL, 2012, Redsea Online Culture Foundation website: accessed on 16/08/2012 www.redsea-online.com

ISWAYDAARSI (EXCHANGE) SERIES

1. *Beerta xayawaanka / Animal Farm*
George Orwell (translated by Maxamed Yuusuf Cartan), 2011.

2. *Essays in honour of Muuse Ismaaciil Galaal*
Edited by Jama Musse Jama, Preface by I M Lewis, 2011.

3. *Anton Chekhov - Sheekooyin la soo xulay (Selected short stories)*
Translated by Siciid Jaamac Xuseen with the help of Rashiid
Sheekh Cabdillaahi "Gadhwayne" and Maxamed Xasan
"Alto", 2011.

4. *Soomaali been ma Maahmaahdo - Somalis do not lie in proverbs*
Georgi Kapchits, 2012.

5. *Maxamed Xaashi Dhamac "Gaarriye"- Biography and Poems*
Edited by Jama Musse Jama, 2012.

BEERTA
XAYAWAANKA

JOORJ ORWEL

Waxa turjumay
M.Y. Cartan

Iswaydaarsi
(Exchange) series No. 1

George Orwell
translated by Maxamed
Yuusuf Cartan
Beerta Xayawaanka
(Animal Farm),
ISBN 9788888934204
Pages 138, Pisa. 2011

George Orwell's "Animal Farm" translated by the late Mohamed Yuusuf Cartan is just published again with copyright permission. The book was one of the literature works that was distributed to the young readers in Somaliland to read in public excerpts during the Moving Library tour which was part of Hargeysa International Book Fair 2011.

The translation of this volume begins a new series of books called "Iswaydaarsi" (exchange) which intends to provide specific knowledge of the international classical literature to the young Somali speaking readership. The Iswaydaarsi series will also include renowned Somali literature translated into foreign language, with the ultimate objective being to harmonize the cultural exchange between written and oral traditions.

Essays in honour of
Muuse Ismaaciil Galaal

Preface of	Contributions by
I. M. Lewis	Anita S. Adam, Sheila Andrzejewski,
Edited by	Georgi Kapchits, Sarah Maguire,
Jama Musse Jama	Martin Orwin, Alexander Zholkovsky

Iswaydaarsi
(Exchange) series No. 2

Essays in honour of Muuse Ismaaciil Galaal
Jama Musse Jama (edited by). Preface of I. M. Lewis
Ponte Invisibile
Pisa, 2011 - ISBN: 9788888934273
Price: 10.00 Euros

Muse Ismail Galaal was researcher, scientist, historian, writer and poet whose most important lasting legacy is the role he played in the creation of the modern written Somali alphabet and written Somali text and in preserving numerous accounts of Somali cultural and heritage, which would otherwise have been lost forever. This is short volume, published in collaboration with Somali Week Festival, is for the commomoration of the 30th anniversary from Musa Ismail Galaal's death.

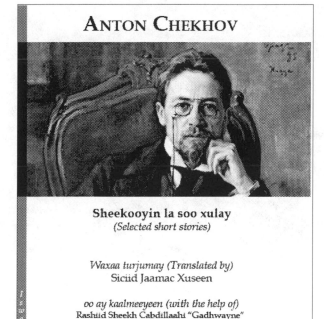

ANTON CHEKHOV

Sheekooyin la soo xulay
(Selected short stories)

Waxaa turjumay *(Translated by)*
Siciid Jaamac Xuseen

oo ay kaalmeeyeen (with the help of)
Rashiid Sheekh Cabdillaahi "Gadhwayne"
iyo Maxamed Xasan Cali "Alto"

PONTE INVISIBILE

Iswaydaarsi
(Exchange) series No. 3

Anton Chekhov - sheekooyin la soo xulay
Waxa turjumay Siciid Jaamac Xuseen
Ponte Invisibile
Pisa, 2011
ISBN: 9788888934280
Price: 12.80 Euros

From the introduction: the essence of this attempt at translating some of Chekhov's short stories has been the fulfilment of the ambitious aim, albeit to a very small degree, of introducing the Somali reader to the cultural world of Chekhov through the glimpses of the realities Anton Chekhov artfully depicts in his own unique style of the world and culture of his time in Russia. See www.redsea-online.com/iswaydaarsi.

Iswaydaarsi
(Exchange) series No. 4

Soomaali been ma maahmaahdo / Somalis do not lie in proverbs
Georgi L. Kapchits
Ponte Invisibile
Pisa, 2012 - ISBN: 9788888934308 Price: 12.80 Euros

Dr Georgi Kapchits' book "Soomaali been ma maahmaahdo-Somalis do not lie in proverbs" based on forty years of work on Somali proverbs. The introduction familiarises the reader with the modern theory of premiology, describes some literary features of Somali proverbs and sayings, and offers their classification, paving the way to the paremiological minimum of the Somali language. The first part of the book presents 249 of the most popular Somali proverbs and proverbial phrases in Somali, with an English translation. The second part provides the reader with several thousand Somali proverbs, the majority of which have been received from oral sources.

JAAMAC MUUSE JAAMAC

Gobannimo bilaash maaha

Hiilka Q∂d∂bka

32

Gogoldhiggii
Cabdiraxmaan Maxamed Cabdillaahi "Cirro"

Qodobka 37ᵃ, xubinta 1ᵃᵃ
Xaqa waxaa loo uunnaa baddan xabaasha hadalka iyo qoraalka, waana mid laga soo horjeeday maamulka Soomaaliyeed...

Curisyo 1

Curisyo (Essays) Series No. 1
Gobannimo bilaash maaha
Jama Musse Jama
Ponte invisibile, Pisa, 2007, ISBN: 88-88934-06-5

The idea behind this publication was to explain to ordinary citizens the significance of Article 32 of the Somaliland constitution, which "guarantees the fundamental right of freedom of expression and makes unlawful all acts to subjugate the press and the media". The book, became part of a wider campaign in conjunction with Somaliland human rights groups for freedom of expression. Gobannimo Bilaash Maaha (roughly translated as 'freedom is not free'), was awarded by the Somaliland Writers' Association. In his book, the author has successfully themed the different levels of freedom, nationality, society, civil liberties and most importantly

Curisyo (Essays) Series No. 2
Ahmed Ibrahim Awale
Qaylo-dhaan deegaan / Environment in crises
Ponte Invisibile, Pisa, 2010, ISBN: 88-88934-13-8
21.00 Euro

Ahmed I. Awale's new book is the first of its type to deal with the highly important issue of environmental disasters, particularly looking at the impact of resource depletion on those whose livelihoods depend on these resources for their survival. Combining academic research with reflections from traditional knowledge, personal philosophies and faith, this book is accessible to a wide range of readers with an interest in Somali culture, the flora and fauna of the Somali regions, and the environmental challenges facing the people who live there. Bilingual in Somali and English, the book is a master piece of work, and is the second book of the Curisyo series.

AHMED IBRAHIM AWALE

QAYLO-DHAAN DEEGAAN
Qoraallo Xulasho ah

ENVIRONMENT IN CRISIS:
Selected Essays with focus on Somali Environment

Curisyo 2

XASAN CABDI MADAR

HIIL
Waayaha dadka la hayb-sooco

Curisyo 3

Curisyo (Essays) Series No. 3
HIIL by Xasan Cabdi Madar
Ponte Invisibile, Pisa, 2010
Price 12,80 Euro

Hassan Abdi Madar's book Hiil (In Defence of/'Hayb-sooco') tackles one of the major issues facing contemporary Somali society in the form of minority rights. It addresses the marginalisation and social exclusion of the 'Gabooye' communities.

Curisyo (Essays) Series No. 4
Adduun iyo taladii
Rashiid Sheekh Cabdillaahi Xaaji Axmed
Ponte Invisibile, Pisa, 2010, ISBN: 9966-7059-16-2
160 pages. Soft cover, 12,80.Euro

Adduun Iyo Taladii is a new book written by Rashid Sheikh Abdillahi 'Gadhwayne' which touches the essence of citizenship. 'Gadhweyne' is a scholar, social scientist, and literary critic. No other book is more at home in the Curis Series than the work of Rashid Sheikh Abdillahi 'Gadhwayne'. In his collection of essays Rashid deals with different aspects of citizenship, which are interconnected and fully complement each other. This book enlightens the reader on various subjects with vital impacts on the building blocks of each society by exploring the themes such as freedom, tolerance, righteousness, equality, and their true normative, ethical, deep moral meaning in the Somali context. It is a work which is inspired by his great sense of social responsibility.

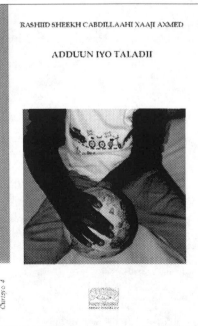

RASHIID SHEEKH CABDILLAAHI XAAJI AXMED

ADDUUN IYO TALADII

Curisyo 4

SICIID JAAMAC XUSEEN

SHUFBEEL

Curisyo ?

Curisyo (Essays) Series No. 5
Shufbeel - tiraab soomaaliyeed
Siciid Jaamac Xuseen
ISBN 88-88934-22-8 EAN 9788888934228
Pages 126, Pisa, 2011

'Shufbeel' is a collection of essays and short stories, including modern and traditional Somali wisdom and entertainment (murti iyo madaddaalo). The author, Saed Jama is one of pilasters for the literary promotion in the Somali speaking society. Shuhbeel is the 5th and latest book of the Curisyo series collection. 'Curisyo' is a series of books, covering a ranging set of topics, yet share the spirit of citizenship. The series so far dealt with several themes, including Freedom of expression, Environment, Tolerence, Ethics, and more.

Curisyo series:

"Curisyo" is series of books published and distributed by Ponte Invisibile (redsea-online.com) and directed by Jama Musse Jama. "Curisyo" series of books contain essays which cover a ranging set of topics, yet share the spirit of citizenship.

Printed in the United States
By Bookmasters